AMOS, OBADIAH, AND JONAH

MESSAGES OF
GOD'S JUSTICE AND MERCY

AMOS, OBADIAH, AND JONAH

MESSAGES OF GOD'S JUSTICE AND MERCY

F. Wayne Mac Leod

Authentic
MEDIA

© 2003 by F. Wayne Mac Leod

00 09 08 07 06 05 04 7 6 5 4 3 2 1
Authentic Lifestyle is an imprint of Authentic Media
PO Box 1047, 129 Mobilization Dr.
Waynesboro, GA 30830 USA
(706) 554-1594
authenticusa@stl.org

ISBN: 1-884543-95-2

Cover design: Paul Lewis

Contents

Obadiah

Jonah

Preface

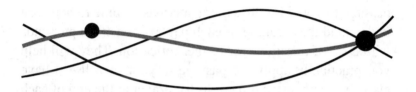

The book of Amos is a prophecy to a nation steeped in materialism. It is the story of a nation who allowed her great blessings to turn her away from the Giver of blessings. It is also the story of a simple shepherd who obediently accepted the call of God and courageously preached God's message to a nation rapidly rushing to ruin. Throughout the prophecy we see the evil effects of the love of possessions and the efforts of a loving God to restore his people to himself.

In the prophecy of Obadiah we meet the Edomites, a self-sufficient, embittered people. We see the results of unresolved conflicts between brothers and its lingering influence on their children. Obadiah is the story of the downfall of a nation because of pride. It is a challenge for us to examine our own differences as brothers and sisters in Christ. It is a reminder of how dependent on God we really are.

Jonah is the story of a man who struggled with the will of God for his life. It is a picture of a loving God who will not forsake his rebellious servant. It shows us how a sovereign God can use our rebellion to accomplish his purposes. It is the story of God's victory through human failure. It is a book that brings encouragement to repentant wanderers and offers hope in a world of sin and despair.

This commentary is not meant to replace the Biblical narrative. It serves only as a guide to take you section by section through the prophecies of Amos, Obadiah, and Jonah. Read the passage indicated at the beginning of each chapter. Ask the Spirit of God to reveal the truth of the passage to you. Use this commentary as a guide to help you understand the meaning of each passage. Each chapter ends with a set of questions for further reflection. They will help you practically apply the passage to your own life. I have also given suggested directions for prayer at the end of each chapter. Once you've finished each section, take a moment to examine your heart and pray through these requests.

My prayer is that this book will be instrumental in helping you walk devotionally through the books of Amos, Obadiah, and Jonah. It is also that you might be encouraged, challenged, and assisted in your daily struggle to live a godly life. May God bless you over the next few weeks as you meditate on these important books from the Old Testament.

F. Wayne Mac Leod

Amos

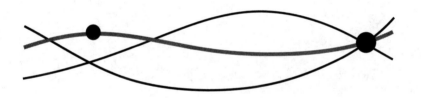

1
Introducing the Prophet

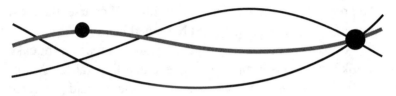

Read Amos 1:1

Before we begin our meditation of Amos' prophecy, it is important that we understand the man and his background. Amos was a shepherd from the region of Tekoa. Tekoa was a somewhat obscure village located approximately fifteen kilometers south of Jerusalem. Verse one leads us to believe that Tekoa was a rural farming community. Thus Amos was not a prophet in the traditional sense nor did he come from a family of prophets (see Amos 7:14). He was a simple shepherd from an obscure farming community, content to live a humble life. Yet it was to this simple man that the Spirit of the Lord came. Unlike the other prophets, he was not professionally trained for this ministry, but he did have a call from God. This was all he needed; it was the source of his power, originality, and authority. It enabled him to move in the power of the Spirit of God, to confidently share with others what God had given him. This is a great challenge to us in our day. Proper education is certainly important, but spiritual authority is paramount. God will often do more through an uneducated shepherd than through an entire community of educated prophets.

Amos means "load" or "burden bearer." It was a name indicative of his role in Israel. He would become the bearer of a heavy burden for the people of God, for the weight of their many sins was crushing them. Ultimately, his heart would be broken for them. This is indeed the way it needed to be. How could he effectively preach if he had no burden? His lack of education meant he could not speak from the great resources of acquired knowledge, so he had no choice but to speak from the great burden the Lord had given him. Of course, the most powerful messages come from burdened hearts.

Amos prophesied two years before a great earthquake shook Israel. This is an important event with regard to Amos. A quick look at his prophecy shows us that he had predicted this earthquake. Look at what he says in chapter 8: "Will not the land tremble for this, and all who live in it mourn? The whole land will rise like the Nile; it will be stirred up and then sink like the river of Egypt" (Amos 8:8). We see it again in chapter nine as he says, "I saw the Lord standing by the altar, and he said: 'Strike the tops of the pillars so that the thresholds shake. Bring them down on the heads of all the people; those who are left I will kill with the sword. Not one will get away, none will escape'" (Amos 9:1).

The picture painted in these verses is of a great earthquake that causes the whole land to tremble. It shakes the pillars of the temple and causes them to come crashing down upon the worshippers. Amos predicted this would take place two years before it actually occurred.

According to the Law of Moses, the sign of a true prophet was the fulfillment of his prophecies. This certainly tells us something about Amos' validity. Since the prophecy was so visibly fulfilled, his credentials were secure. Though he may not have been educated in the right school, and though he did not come from a family of prophets, he carried great authority and was to be taken very seriously. He was a true prophet of God.

It is also of importance to look at what was happening in the land of Israel during the life of Amos. Amos prophesied during the reign of king Uzziah of Judah and Jeroboam, king of Israel. King Uzziah was considered to be good king. Under his reign, God gave the nation peace and prosperity. He successfully ridded Judah of some of her most bitter enemies. He also fortified Jerusalem, increased the size and strength of his army, and undertook many significant agricultural projects. Judah was a respected nation under Uzziah and his fame spread throughout the region. This period of Judah's history closely resembles the period of great national power during the reigns of David and Solomon.

As for Jeroboam, while he was not considered to be a good king, the nation of Israel was still experiencing prosperity. Jeroboam reigned longer than any other king of Israel. He was successful in restoring territory that had been taken from them during the reigns of previous kings. The nation was safe, secure, and wealthy.

The question needs to be asked: Why does Amos prophesy at a time like this? Why speak words of destruction at a time when God was obviously blessing his people? It is precisely because of this prosperity that Israel and Judah needed to hear the message of Amos. Their prosperity had caused them to feel secure in themselves (see 6:1). Their wealth had caused them to become complacent and spiritually weak. King Uzziah of Judah had become arrogant because of his prosperity, and the nation itself was guilty of oppressing and neglecting the poor (see 4:1).

Verse one is loaded with meaning. From this verse alone we catch a glimpse of the character and personality of Amos. We learn that he is a man called of God to address a people living in a situation not unlike our own. His authority is unquestionable and qualifies him to speak to his people as

God's representative. That same call qualifies him to speak to us as well. May we pay close attention to what he says.

For Consideration:

- Why do we consider education and credentials to be so important in our age? How important are they with regard to God's call?

- What qualifications does Amos have for ministry?

- What is the danger of materialism?

- Have you ever found yourself attempting ministry by yourself and pushing God aside? What is the result of this pride?

- Where would you be today if it were not for God's activity in your life?

- What in particular takes your attention away from the Lord God?

For Prayer:

- Have you ever hesitated to move out in obedience because you did not consider yourself qualified? Ask God to forgive you and to give you the boldness and confidence to step out in his strength.

- Ask God to open your eyes to the things that seem to distract you from him.

- Thank the Lord for each blessing by name that he has given you. Take a few moments to consider his goodness in your life.

- Ask the Lord to show you more and more just how dependent you are upon him.

2

Judgment against the Nations

Read Amos 1:2–2:5

In the last meditation we were introduced to the prophet Amos; now we will look at his message. Verse 2 begins his message with a proclamation of the coming of the Lord to judge. The Lord is pictured in verse 2 as a great warrior coming out of Jerusalem to judge the nations. As he advances, he roars like a great lion. Peals of thunder follow him. The pastures dry up and the tops of the mountains wither all around him. This is no ordinary warrior who comes out of Zion. This is the great and terrifying God of the universe. He is coming to bring his accusations against the nations.

Notice that each of the accusations begins with the expression: "for three sins . . . even for four." What does this expression mean? It appears to be a common expression used in Amos' day to say that these nations multiplied sin in their lives. The point, then, is that they are guilty beyond a reasonable doubt. Let's examine the accusations of this great warrior-judge against the nations of the day.

God begins by laying out his charges against the city of Damascus in Syria. He accuses her of threshing Gilead with "sledges having iron teeth." A sledge was an instrument used to separate grain from the straw. It was made of wood and had sharp stones (in this case iron teeth) on the bottom. Oxen drew the sledge over the field of cut grain, a process which split the straw husks and allowed the grain to be harvested. So God is saying that Damascus had threshed God's people like an ox threshing the grain. He would not let this crime go unpunished.

Because of their crime against his people, God tells the inhabitants of Damascus that he will send a fire on the house of Hazael, the king of the city. Now Hazael lived during the time of the prophet Elisha; in fact, he visited Elisha to inquire about the future of his son Ben-Hadad who was sick. When Elisha saw him, God revealed to him what this king would do to the people of Israel. Elisha wept at this revelation, and Hazael inquired as to the reason:

> "Why is my lord weeping?" asked Hazael. "Because I know the harm you will do to the Israelites," he answered. "You will set fire to their fortified places, kill their young men with the sword, dash their little children to the ground, and rip open their pregnant women." (2 Kings 8:12)

We see in Amos that God promises to judge the household of Hazael because of the evil that he had done to Israel. He would send the fire of judgment upon his family even judging Ben-Hadad for the crimes of his father. Though powerful, his fortresses would not protect him on the day of God's wrath. Ben-Hadad and his people would be left defenseless before the great warrior-God of Israel. The gate of the great city of Damascus would be broken down. God would enter the city and bring it to utter ruin.

The kings of the Valley of Aven and Beth Eden in Syria would also be held accountable to God for what they had done to God's people. The inhabitants of Aram, a city-state closely connected to Damascus, would be sent into exile because of their sin. They would lose everything because they had turned their back on God and harmed his people.

We learn from this that there is a very close and personal relationship between God and his people. To disrespect or intentionally harm God's people is to disrespect God himself. God is swift to judge such crimes. God's judgment of Damascus should remind us that we need to be very careful in how we treat God's children.

Attention now shifts from Damascus in Syria to Gaza, a city southwest of Jerusalem in the region of Philistia. God accuses Gaza of taking whole communities of Israelites captive and selling them to Edom. The Philistines cared nothing for their captives; they were concerned only for what they could get out of them. The Lord God despised this practice of selling his people into slavery because it reduced the objects of his love to mere commodities to be bought and sold for profit. We can only wonder what God thinks of us in our modern commercial age where we see people as a means to make a profit. Let us be warned by the sentence God hands out to the Philistines because of their sin.

God promises that he will set fire to the walls of Gaza. Just as they had attacked the Israelites and burnt down their city walls, so it would be done to them. With their walls burnt down, they would have no defense against their enemies. They would be treated as they had treated others. They would be powerless to stop an attack. All the wealth they had accumulated would be plundered and they would be slaughtered by their enemies.

Verse 8 tells us that the Philistine kings Ashdod and Ashkelon would also be destroyed. They too would be judged for their inhuman treatment of God's people. As leaders, they would be held individually accountable to God. They would suffer the consequences of their evil ways.

God's hand would also be turned against the inhabitants of the city of Ekron. One by one they too would perish. God's judgment would not stop until all of the Philistines were dead. The sentence was severe, but it was just. They would perish because they had not respected God's people.

The next people to be sentenced are the people of Tyre (1:9–10). Notice that they are guilty of the same sin as the Philistines. They too had sold whole communities of Israelites into slavery to the Edomites. In so doing they had further sinned in that they disregarded their treaty of brotherhood with the Israelites. What is this treaty of brotherhood? Some commentators believe it is a reference to the days of Solomon, for according to 1 Kings 5:1–12, King Hiram of Tyre helped Solomon build the temple of the Lord. Here in Amos chapter 1, however, we see that the people of Tyre had betrayed Israel and willingly sold them into slavery to enrich their own pockets. Is this not a parallel to what happened to our Lord when Judas betrayed him for twenty pieces of silver? Is not the betrayal of a friend worse than the insult of an enemy? God would justly punish the people of Tyre for selling their friends into slavery to the Edomites. Notice too that the punishment of Tyre would be the same as the punishment of Gaza. Her walls would be burnt down and she would be left without defenses.

Edom is the next nation on the list (1:1–12). We have already seen that they were guilty of buying Israelite slaves. One would think that this would be the central focus of God's sentence against them, but it was only one of their many crimes. Amos draws our attention to a greater crime: they pursued their brothers with the sword and showed no compassion.

Remember that the Edomites were the descendants of Esau, the brother of Jacob, which made them cousins to the

Israelites. This makes their crime of buying Israelite slaves even more hideous. Now from the very beginning there had been hatred between these two families. According to Amos, the hatred of Edom raged continuously. Their fury ran unchecked. Edom had no desire to make things right with Israel and chose to live in hatred and bitterness. For this, God promised to send the fire of his judgment against them. The cities of Teman and Bozrah would be destroyed. The whole nation would be placed under the judgment of God.

Where is the nation of Edom today? It does not exist. Its name has been forgotten. By refusing to be reconciled, Edom brought God's wrath upon itself. The same thing will happen to those who choose to allow the flame of bitterness and hatred to blaze within their lives. Is there someone in your life that you are refusing to forgive? Is there a brother or sister in your life with whom you need to be reconciled? If God is speaking to you about this matter, learn a lesson from Edom. Cast aside the bitterness and be reconciled before you face God's judgment.

The nation of Ammon falls next on the list of nations to be judged (1:13–15). Ammon's crime was one of greed. They were willing to rip open pregnant women with the sword if, by doing so, they could extend their borders. In the name of greed, people were slaughtered. What a horrible thing! Greed stops at nothing to satisfy its evil desires. It has a tendency to grow in intensity and overwhelm the people inflicted by it.

God hates greed and would punish Ammon for it. The fire of God's wrath would consume their possessions. Like a violent wind, God would fall upon them and sweep them away. Ammon's king and her officials would go into exile and be held at the mercy of their enemies. Their land and their possessions would be taken from them. Their greed would forever remain unsatisfied.

In chapter 2, Moab stands before God to receive her

sentence. Moab was guilty of burning the bones of the king of Edom. Even though Edom was certainly not living according to the purposes of God, Moab had no right to take it on themselves to deal with the king of Edom. By burning his bones they showed disrespect for God. Even though Edom deserved to be judged because they had pursued Israel with the sword, Moab was not justified in desecrating the bones of their king. In this we should be reminded of David, who patiently waited for God's timing with King Saul. He had many opportunities to kill his enemy, but he refused to do so because God had given Saul his position of authority. He respected the decision of a sovereign God though he did not understand his ways. Moab did just the opposite. Because of their crime, Moab's fortresses would be destroyed. The nation would fall amid the noise of great tumult and the blast of a war trumpet. Their own king would perish and they would be left without a leader and without defenses.

There is an important lesson for us here. While we may never be guilty of literally burning the bones of an evil king, we could easily be guilty of harsh and critical words against leaders that the Lord has placed over us. They may not deserve our confidence. They may be wrong in their methods. They may even be evil. This, however, does not justify our criticism or rebellion. Moab should serve as a lesson for how careful we need to be in our relationship with those whom God has seen fit to place in authority over us.

The last nation discussed in this section is the nation of Judah (2:4–5). While the crimes of the other nations were crimes against their fellow man, Judah's crime was against God. Her punishment, however, would be just as severe as the punishment of the pagan nations. Judah had rejected God's law. She had turned her back on the true God and worshipped idols. For this, God would not hesitate to send the fire of his judgment upon her. Jerusalem would be consumed by fire. Though they were God's people, Judah too would have to answer to God for her actions.

It is somewhat surprising that God's people are included in the list of pagan nations to be judged. God has accused the foreign nations of mistreating their fellow man (1:3), profiting from enslaving each other (1:6), betraying friendships (1:9), not forgiving their brothers and sisters (1:11), greed (1:13), and disrespect for leaders (2:1). The questions for us to ask are these: Is the church of our day free from such practices? Is there any difference between our churches and the secular workplace? Do our churches stand out as beacons of righteousness amidst the darkness of the world around them? The words of God that Amos gave to the Israelites are to be given to us as well. He calls us to examine our own lives through the examples set before us in these two chapters.

Take some time right now to review what we have learned in this passage. Examine your heart and your relationships with the people in your life. Are you guilty of any of these crimes? If so, confess them to God. He will cleanse you and give you victory over your sin if you turn to him in repentance.

For Consideration:

- Are Christians better in their relationships than unbelievers? Why or why not?

- Compare what we have seen here in this chapter with your own nation or church. What would God say to your nation or church today?

- Why do you suppose there are so many conflicts between believers in the church today?

- What does this passage tell us about the attitude we need to have toward our leaders?

- What do we learn from this passage about the feelings of God toward his people?

For Prayer:

- Search your own heart to see if you have any relationships that need mending.

- Is there someone you have problems relating to? Ask the Lord to help you deal with this person with the love of Christ.

- Take a moment to pray for your nation or church. Ask God to heal those things that need healing.

- Ask God to forgive you for the times you have not been sensitive to his people and the leadership he has established over you.

- Ask the Lord to restore unity in his church.

3
Judgment against Israel

Read Amos 2:6–16

In the last meditation we examined the judgments of God upon seven different nations. It is now Israel's turn to be judged and she faces a threefold accusation from God. Let's examine these in detail.

First, God accuses his people of injustice and greed. Notice in verse 6 that they sold the righteous for silver and the needy for a pair of sandals. The word *righteous* in the Hebrew simply refers to a law-abiding citizen, but it should be remembered that the law of the Israelites was also the law of God. What is the significance of this then? The Israelites are guilty of the same crime as Edom (1:6) and Tyre (1:9). Israel was profiting from the filthy practice of enslaving the innocent.

In verse 7 Israel is accused of trampling the heads of the poor just as they might trample the dust of the ground. The New King James Version says, "They pant after the dust of the earth which is on the head of the poor." This means they had no compassion or concern for the needy. Their conscience did not seem to prick them. They would step on a poor man as quickly as they would step on the dust of the earth. If he had something they wanted, they would devise means of taking it from him to benefit themselves. Not only were they trampling the poor, this verse also tells us that they denied justice to the oppressed. The judges of the nation had become concerned only with those who had money. As for the poor and needy, however, there was no profit in defending them. They were cast aside and denied justice.

As God looked upon Israel he saw people throughout the land lying down beside their pagan altars on garments taken in pledges. The wine they drank in the house of their gods had been taken as fines from those they oppressed. They profited from the misfortune of the needy. They filled their pockets with money taken in fines. They clothed themselves with clothes taken from those who could not keep up with their heavy requirements. Notice how they felt no shame in doing this. They took these objects to the houses of the pagan gods and used them in their religious festivities. The entire nation was guilty of injustice, greed, and idolatry.

Second, God's people were guilty of immorality (verse 7). Amos points out that a father and son would have sexual relations with the same girl. While it is clear that the verse speaks of a sexual relationship, it is unclear as to the age of the female referred to in this passage. The word *girl* in the original language refers to a female who is usually anywhere in age from infancy to adolescence. It is possible that the passage is actually referring to incest in which the *girl* being referred to is directly related to the males. It may also refer to the practice of religious prostitution that was common among the pagan religions of the day. What is clear, however, is that the moral standard God had established in his Word was being violated. Marriage and sexuality were being abused and as such, the name of God was being dishonored. Remember that these are the children of God who are so flagrantly violating God's commandments.

Third, the people of Israel were guilty of turning their backs to God despite his rich blessings. In verse 9 God calls his people to consider all the great things he had done for them. He calls them to remember how he had destroyed the Amorites who stood between God's people and the Promised Land. Though they were as tall as cedar trees and as strong as great oaks, God destroyed the Amorites and gave his people the Promised Land. These enemies were completely annihilated like trees chopped down and completely uprooted, and would never pose a threat to God's people again.

God also reminds his people of the time they spent in bondage in Egypt. He reminds them how he delivered them from the cruelty of the Egyptian Pharaohs. He reminds them of how he cared for them during the forty years they wandered through the wilderness. He reminds them of how he led them to the land of the Amorites and gave them that land—the land he had promised their forefathers. Never once did he fail them as a people.

God also raised up prophets and Nazarites from among the Israelites. These prophets and Nazarites entered into an intimate relationship with God. The Nazarites took special vows of consecration to the Lord. They promised to live for him and to abstain from wine and strong drink. They also refused to cut their hair as a sign of their separation unto God. These people were to be honored in Jewish society, but notice Israel's response to them. They showed no respect at all. They made the Nazarites drink wine, thus making them guilty of violating their vows to God. As for the prophets, they were ordered to prophesy no longer. The people of Israel cared nothing about what God had to say to them. They completely disregarded his Word.

What would be the judgment for this threefold crime against God? Israel would be punished because of their disobedience and disregard for God and his Word. Like a cart weighed down with sheaves, so God was weighed down by their sin (verse 13). The heavy hand of God's discipline would come upon them. No one would escape judgment. The swift would not be swift enough. The strong would not be strong enough. The warrior would not be able to defend himself. The archer would not be able to stand his ground. All would be forced to run from the fierce combat as the enemy flooded their ranks. He who sought to escape on foot and he who mounted a horse to retreat would both be caught and suffer the judgment of God. Even the bravest of all the warriors would flee in terror. Israel would be helpless in the day of God's wrath. No one would escape.

This passage reminds us that even the people of God will one day have to answer for the decisions they make during their lives. What will be our response to God on that day? We will not be able to hide our sins. We will not be strong enough or swift enough to avoid this judgment. Our only defense is to come to him for cleansing before we are judged. Forgiveness can be ours if we confess our sins now. The blood of Christ is sufficient to cover all of our sins but we must claim that forgiveness before it's too late.

For Consideration:

- God's people have been accused of greed, immorality, and despising his prophets. Are these crimes found in our land today? Give some examples of this.

- Could God be speaking to the church of our day in these verses? Explain.

- What are the obstacles that stand between you and God today? God demonstrated to his people that though the Amorites were taller than cedars they would be cut down and uprooted. Can God do this for you today? Can he cut down and pull up by the roots those things that stand between you and him?

For Prayer:

- Ask God to send a spirit of repentance to our land.

- Ask God to forgive you for the times when you showed disrespect for those he has placed in authority over you.

- Ask God to reveal to you what it is that stands between you and him. Ask him to pull it up by the roots.

- Thank the Lord that he is a God of justice and that he will judge sin even if it is among his very own people.

4

You Alone Have I Chosen

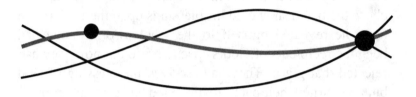

Read Amos 3:1–15

One of the most difficult things we can ever have to deal with on this earth is the betrayal of a loved one. The fact that we have given ourselves to a person and sacrificed much for them makes the pain of their betrayal all the more devastating. God experienced such pain in his relationship with his people in the days of Amos, but he still sought to reconcile with them.

Amos begins this section of his prophecy by calling his people to listen to the word God has for them. God begins in verse 1 by reminding his people of how he had brought them out of the land of Egypt where they had suffered tremendously. They had been beaten and oppressed under the cruel Egyptian domination. They had been reduced to slavery to serve the Egyptian tyrants. At one point, Pharaoh actually ordered the death of all the male Israelite children. Thousands of infants were murdered or thrown into the Nile as Pharaoh sought to rid the nation of what he perceived to be a threat to his reign. These were days that would never be forgotten by the Jews, for it was into this situation that the Lord God sent his servant Moses. Through this chosen instrument, God revealed his power and miraculously delivered his people from their oppressors. God calls on his people to recall this event and return to him.

Verse 2 then tells us that this nation of Israel was the nation God had chosen from among all the families of the earth. He could have chosen any nation he wanted. God knew they would be rebellious from the start, yet he still chose them and showered his blessings upon them. Through them he revealed himself to the whole world. They had been the recipients of God's special grace but now they had rejected that grace. They had received the blessing of God but now turned their backs to him. God had sent his prophets to warn them. They had been given his revelation but now refused it. This justified their punishment.

If you are reading this commentary you are very likely the type of person who claims to love the Lord. You are aware of his blessings in your life. You have access to the Word of God and books such as this that illuminate it. You are in a very similar situation to Israel. To turn your back on the revelation you have been given is a very serious matter. 2 Peter 2:21 says that it would be better for you to never to have known the way of righteousness than to know it and reject it. There is a special responsibility placed upon your shoulders.

From this opening statement, God proceeds to a series of rhetorical questions. Let's look briefly at these questions.

The first question from verse 3 is, "Do two walk together unless they agree to do so?" When you see two people walking together down the street on a hot summer day you could safely assume that they have agreed to do so. It would only be under rare circumstances that people would be forced to walk together against their will. The answer to this question is very obvious.

The second question (verse 4) was equally obvious to the minds of the people of Amos' day, "Does a lion roar in the thicket when he has no prey?" The imagery here is of a lion in search of food. As a hunter it would be foolish for the lion to announce his presence in the forest by roaring as he searched for his prey. On the contrary, the lion approaches his enemy in the utmost silence. It is only when he is almost on top of his prey that he dares to let out a roar. The second part of the question is, "Will the lion growl in his den if he has not caught his prey?" A hungry lion is a lion in search of food. When the lion is hungry he will not stay in his den. He will go out in search of his prey. As long as he is in search of prey he will not be making any unnecessary noise. Again this question would not tax the brains of God's people.

Following along in the hunting imagery the third question (verse 5) asks, "Does a bird fall into a trap on the ground when there is no bait on the trap?" If you set a trap for a bird, the first thing you need to do is find something that will attract the bird to the place where you have set the trap. You will probably put some birdseed or food of some kind to attract the bird. In order for the trap to work you must find a way of getting the bird to come to it.

The fourth question comes from the same verse and also relates to the imagery of a trap, "Does a trap spring when there is nothing to catch?" Have you ever set a mousetrap? What would you think if one night you were sleeping and awoke to the sound of the trap springing shut? Would the assumption not be that something was caught in your trap? The trap will not close until there is something to close it.

The fifth question (verse 6) is, "When the trumpet sounds in the city do not the people tremble?" The trumpet in Bible times was sounded as a warning of the approaching enemy. If you lived in Bible times and you heard the sound of a trumpet, what would be your response? Your response would be to gather your children into your house, lock the doors, and pray to God for safety. Or you might gather your possessions and flee with your family to a safe place. You would certainly tremble in fear.

What is the purpose of all of these questions? The purpose seems to be to lead us to the final, very important question, "When disaster comes to the city has not the Lord caused it?" (verse 6). Even as the answer to all the above questions is obvious, so it is with this question. There can be no doubting that if disaster came to the city, the Lord God had allowed it to take place. Nothing can happen without the permission of a sovereign God. If God desired, he could stop all calamities. What the Lord is telling his people is that disaster would come, and when it did, God wanted his people to realize that he brought it upon them because of their sin.

Verse 7 goes on to tell us that God does nothing without revealing his plans to his servants the prophets. He does not need to reveal his plans to his prophets, but he does for a very important reason: God does not delight in bringing calamity upon his people (Joel 2:13). He reveals his plans so his people might repent of their sins and escape his judgment. He is a God of mercy and forgiveness.

In verse 8 God reminds his people that the lion of his judgment has already roared. We have seen that the lion only roars when it is on top of its prey. The judgment of God is already upon Israel like the lion pouncing upon his prey.

Verse 8 goes on to say that since the sovereign God had spoken, his prophets could now prophesy. It is never easy to announce bad news. Amos found no secret pleasure in letting his people know that the judgment of God was upon them. He could not hold back this word, however. When God spoke to him and revealed his purposes, Amos was forced to share this matter with his people. The challenge of this verse is this: When you know that the judgment of God is coming, how can you not warn those who are under that judgment? What kind of person would simply watch a child run out onto a busy street without calling out to warn him? What kind of person would let a friend or neighbor enter eternity without God and not seek to warn them of the danger of refusing Christ's forgiveness? Yes, God has spoken in his Word. He has revealed his plan and his judgment upon this sinful world. He has also revealed a plan of escape in the Lord Jesus, his Son. Can we keep this message to ourselves? When God has spoken, who can help but share that message with others? Amos, like you and me, was obligated to share his knowledge with others with the hope that some would be saved.

In verse 9, a proclamation goes out to the people of Ashdod and Egypt to assemble in Samaria, the capital of Israel. Why were they to assemble here? The verse goes on to tell us that they were to assemble to see what was happening among the people of God. Notice that there was great unrest among the people of God. They were guilty of oppressing each other. Egypt, in particular, would have a difficult time understanding why God's people would oppress each other. Their God had delivered them from Egyptian oppression only to see them oppressing each other. Egypt is called to act as a witness against the people of God.

Verse 10 tells us that the people of God did not know what was right. Even though they had the prophets and the written Word of God, they chose to disregard it and wandered off in sin and rebellion. Because of their guilt, God would send an enemy to rule over the land (verse 11). The land God had given to his people would be taken from them. Their rebellion had driven a wedge between them and their blessings. Their strongholds would be pulled down; their fortresses would be plundered.

In verse 12 Amos paints a very vivid picture for us. The picture is of a lion that has pounced upon a sheep. The shepherd has come too late. By the time he arrives and chases away the lion, all that is left of the sheep is two leg bones and a piece of an ear. This is what would happen to

Israel. There would be no one there to save them. All that would remain of Israel would be the broken remains of a once glorious nation.

The second half of verse twelve is very difficult to understand. Bible translators are uncertain as to how to translate this verse from the Hebrew. The New Revised Standard Version reads, "Thus says the LORD: As the shepherd rescues from the mouth of the lion two legs, or a piece of an ear, so shall the people of Israel who live in Samaria be rescued, with the corner of a couch and part of a bed." The idea is that all that would remain of their wealth would be a corner of a couch and a part of a bed. Like the mutilated sheep, there would be nothing of value left when God finished judging his people.

Amos is called upon to proclaim this judgment upon God's people. The day of her punishment was coming. On that day, God would destroy their altars in Bethel. *Bethel* means "house of God." This city, however, had become anything but a house of God. Now it was filled with evil and sin. The horns God had commanded to be placed on the altar would be sawn off. What had once been a place of refuge from an enemy would no longer be available. This is indicative of the inability of the people to flee from God's wrath. There would be no safe haven.

Notice in verse 15 that their fancy summer and winter houses (adorned with ivory) and their mansions would be demolished in the day of God's wrath. When the enemies came into Israel, they would destroy everything in the land. They would set it on fire and leave nothing but a pile of ruins.

This chapter is a real warning to those of us who claim to know the Lord. It reminds me of what Jesus tells us in the gospel of Luke, ". . . from everyone who has been given much, much will be demanded; and from the one who has been entrusted with much, much more will be asked." We, of all people, have received great blessing from the Lord. Added blessing means added responsibility. May the Lord help us to be faithful.

For Consideration:

- In what way has the Lord blessed you? Take a moment to consider what he has done in your life.

- Has your service to God been equal to his blessing? When you stand before God will you hear him say, "Well done"? What in particular needs to be changed in your life to make you a better servant?

- In this chapter we see that Amos could not stop himself from sharing what God had revealed to him. What is it that keeps us from sharing our faith with others?

- Have you ever met believers who believe that they can live the way they want now that they have been forgiven by the Lord? What does this passage have to say to these believers?

For Prayer:

- Take a moment to thank the Lord for his blessings in your life.

- Ask the Lord to give you the boldness of Amos to share what God has done for you.

- Confess any shortcomings in your relationship with God and ask him to enable you to be a servant in whom he would be proud.

5

The Discipline of God

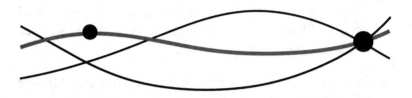

Read Amos 4:1–13

Have you ever met a child who stubbornly persists in his defiant ways? It seems that no matter how much the child is disciplined, he continues to get into trouble. He never seems to learn his lesson. This is the complaint of God against his people. Though he had been disciplining them, God's people continued in their evil ways.

In verse 1, God speaks out against the women who crushed and oppressed the poor and needy. Notice here that God calls these women "cows of Bashan." The region of Bashan was noted for its green pastures, ideal territory for cattle (Psalm 22:12 and Ezekiel 39:18). In Bashan, cows lived in the lap of luxury. It is for this reason that God compares the women of Samaria to the cows of Bashan. The Samaritan women were drunk with luxury and excess. Like the cows of Bashan, they had everything they could ever have wanted, yet they were never satisfied. They constantly cried out for more. To satisfy the cravings of their wives, their husbands would oppress the poor and crush the needy.

God was not pleased with their actions and speaks out against the rich who oppressed the poor. He warns them that they will be taken away with hooks. Like a fish removed from its natural habitat, so God's people would be removed from their land and their blessings.

In fact, they would go out of their land through the breaches in the walls. The imagery here is of a city wall that has been violently attacked by an enemy. Instead of walking through the city gate, they would be led out through the holes the enemies had knocked in their walls. This is an image of defeat and humiliation.

In verses 4 and 5, the Lord uses irony to further communicate to his people. It should be understood that the Lord is not commanding his people to follow these commands but is ridiculing his people for their foolishness. By means of these two verses the Lord lets his people know that he is aware of their evil ways. In verse 4 God tells his people to go to Bethel and sin. Ironically, Bethel means "house of God," for at one time it housed the Ark of the Covenant. Both Abraham and Jacob worshipped God in Bethel (Genesis 35). Under King Jeroboam, Bethel became a worship center for the calf god he set up in opposition to the God of his fathers (1 Kings 12:25–33). In verse 4, God also tells his people to go to Gilgal and sin even more. In Gilgal, Joshua renewed his covenant with God by circumcising the men who had come with him through the wilderness. Using Gilgal as a military base, he conquered the Promised Land. Hosea tells us, however, that Gilgal became a very wicked city (Hosea 9:15). Like Bethel, it had become a haven of sin. These two cities were at one time the center of God's activity, but now they turned their backs to him and became known for their evil and rebellion. God's people were following the example of Bethel and Gilgal. God tells them to go to these cities because, like them, they would be judged for their sin. This verse is not so much a command of God as it is a sentence of judgment.

The second statement God makes here is, "Bring your sacrifices every morning, your tithes every three years and your leavened bread." Despite the fact that the Israelites were following the evil ways of Bethel and Gilgal, they were still tithing to the Levites every three years according to God's command in Deuteronomy 14:28, "At the end of every three years, bring all the tithes of that year's produce and store it in your towns."

God's people, despite their rebellion against him, were faithfully bringing their tithes and offerings to him. Notice, however, that the bread they brought was leavened bread. This was defiled bread. Any bread brought to the Lord needed to be unleavened (without yeast). Yeast or leaven was a symbol of sin. Their offerings were unclean.

Why were they bringing their offerings to the house of God when they were living in rebellion against him? Notice that God saw through their outward actions to their hidden attitudes. He saw that they were not bringing their offerings for him but for themselves. He saw how they boasted and bragged about how much they gave (verse 5). They were giving only to be seen by others. They were not giving out of love for God but out of proud, self-seeking hearts.

In the remainder of the chapter, God shows his people what had been happening to their land because of their rebellion against him. There was an economic decline in the land. Peculiar things were happening in nature. The earth failed to produce crops. One field had enough rain while another withered away. People had no resources to provide for their basic needs of food and water. God was trying to use these painful circumstances to get their attention, but his people did not recognize that God was speaking to them. They continued to rebel. They refused to return to him.

How many people around us today are thirsty for Living Water? They drink deeply from the water the world offers them but find that they leave as thirsty as they came. Reports abound of men and women who have drunk deeply of the well of worldly pleasure, fame, and riches but have been left barren and parched. Their souls are not satisfied. Why do they not turn to the Lord?

As the passage continues, God further seeks the attention of his people. "I struck your gardens and vineyards," he says in verse 9. Everything around them was filled with blight and mildew. Locusts devoured their fig and olive trees. Catastrophe after catastrophe fell upon the people of God, yet they would not hear his voice. God also used plagues and destruction to try to get their attention (verse 10). Young men were killed. Horses were lost in battle. The stench of rotting corpses filled the air in their camp. God was speaking to his people but they were deaf to his voice.

Whole cities were overthrown in a similar manner to that of Sodom and Gomorrah (verse 11). God's people knew the story of the overthrow of these two cities, but they could not seem to understand that God was doing the same thing to them. They could not see how the story of these two cities had anything to do with them. In God's judgment they were left like a burning stick rescued from the fire. What good is a burning stick rescued from the fire? You cannot use it for building anything. The charred remains of the stick are good for nothing but to be thrown back into the fire. This was a metaphor of God's people. They had been humbled before the world, yet they did not listen to what God was saying to them. Instead they stubbornly persisted in their sin and rebellion.

We are left here to wonder how blind these people really were to the things of God. How could they no longer see God in what was happening around them? How could they feel that as long as they were bringing their sacrifices and tithes to the temple, things would be all right? How could they continue to live their lives as they wanted with very little concern for God and his purposes?

God told his people what would happen to them because of their rebellion against him. He called them to prepare for his judgment. This meeting is not the type of meeting that those who love and serve the Lord will experience. This meeting is the meeting between sinful men and a righteous God. The day was coming when these sinners would meet the one who formed the mountains, created the wind, turned the dawn into darkness, and knows the thoughts of man. There was nothing they could hide from him. The day was coming when the Almighty God himself, the one who treads the high places of the earth, would enter into judgment against these religious hypocrites. It would be a fearful day.

For Consideration:

- How much of what we do has as its motive to please men or glorify self? Why is this so wrong?

- Do you see evidence of God speaking to our society today? What do you suppose God is saying to our present-day society through this evidence?

- Compare this chapter with present-day "religion." What are the similarities?

- Do you have ears to hear what the Lord is saying to you? How does God speak to us in our day? Have we been listening?

- Do you know individuals who are living in false security? What are they trusting in?

For Prayer:

- Ask God to give you ears to hear and eyes to see what he is saying through circumstances around us today.

- If you have been guilty of seeking the approval of man over the approval of God, take a moment to confess your sin. Ask God to give you victory in this matter.

- Take a moment to pray for those around you who have been living with false security. Ask the Lord to reveal himself to them before it is too late.

6

Seek Me and Live

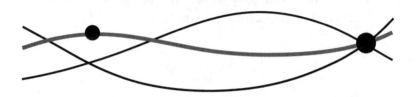

Read Amos 5:1–17

In chapter 4 we saw how God had been trying to get the attention of his people through disorder in the natural environment and how they had consistently refused to listen to him. The result of this blindness is revealed in chapter 5. The nation of Israel is once again called to listen to the word of the Lord, for he is about to sing a lament concerning his people.

A lament is a song of mourning, and the Lord begins by singing about Virgin Israel. Why does God speak of Israel as a virgin when it is clear that she is anything but pure? The answer seems to lie in the fact that she was like a young woman with a whole life ahead of her. As a young woman, however, she fell into foul iniquity, never to rise again. While it is a horrible thing to see the death of any human being, when the life of a young person is snuffed out, the tragedy is amplified. God laments because Israel is like a young woman gone astray. He laments that she will be deserted in her own land with no one to lift her or help her in her dying hours. He laments her abandonment. Where is the justice of God in this? Why would he lament but not save? From chapter 4 we see that the reason these things are happening to God's people is because they have persistently and rebelliously refused to listen to God. They are receiving the just reward for their sin.

Notice in verse 3 that the blessing of God would be removed from the Israelite army. When their army marched out with a thousand men to fight against their enemies, they would return with only a hundred. When they marched out with a hundred they would return with only ten. They would be powerless against their enemies. Is this not what disobedience to God will do to a church or an individual? Our sin acts as a barrier between God and us. Have you been powerless in your spiritual walk? Has your church been getting nowhere? Does the picture of this Israelite army describe your life? Maybe it is time for you to search your heart and life to be sure that you are not blocking the supply of God's blessing by your sin.

In verse 4 God calls upon his people to seek him and live, a command he will repeat in verses 6 and 14. This is a very important statement, for it is not the desire of God to see his people in such a pathetic state. Now, there are those who have come to believe that powerlessness in the Christian life is the normal experience. They become used to producing no fruit and having very few answers to prayer. Many times they feel that death and fruitlessness are normal for the Christian. God is saying just the opposite. He is inviting the rebellious and the cynical to seek him and live. He is inviting them to experience vitality and victory in their walk with him. This can only happen, however, as they seek him, and seeking God implies a turning from sin, self-effort, and the world. This is something that the people of God in Amos' day hesitated to do. Living in a materialistic society with many blessings around them, they were not really sure that they wanted to give up these things.

Notice here that seeking God implied that God's people would cease from seeking Bethel and going to Gilgal and Beersheba. Amos 4:4 tells us that while Bethel and Gilgal had been the centers of God's activity at one time, these towns had now turned their backs to God. Now they were known for their rebellion against him. If God's people were going to seek him, it meant separating themselves from the evil places and practices in their lives. Seeking God was their only means of escape from the terrible judgment that was to come upon them. If they did not seek God he would sweep through them like a fire. Bethel and Gilgal would be reduced to nothing (verse 5). When the fire of God's judgment came upon them, there would be nothing they could do to reverse it. Their destiny would be sealed.

In verse 7 God tells his people that he would come in judgment against those who turned justice into bitterness. Justice was made bitter because they had corrupted it. It was bitter because they despised it. They preferred to profit at the expense of the poor. They preferred to twist the justice system to meet their own needs. God's people had cast righteousness to the ground as if it were garbage.

As if to emphasize the foolishness of God's people, Amos reminds them of the God they were rebelling against. He is seen here as the God who aligned the constellations of Pleiades and Orion. He is the one who turned the blackness of the night into dawn and who darkens the light of day to make night. He is the one who poured water down upon the earth in the form of rain to fill the oceans. This was also the God who would bring judgment upon his people. This was a God to be feared. How foolish it was to stir up his wrath!

This great and awesome God would flash destruction like lightning upon the strongholds of the land. This destruction would come quickly and without hesitation. The people would not be able to escape. Their fortified cities would be laid waste. God would do this because his people hated those who stood for justice in their courts, because they despised the honest people of the land, and because they trampled the poor and forced them to pay what they could not afford to pay. Their luxurious stone houses would be taken from them. Their lush vineyards would no longer produce crops. The blessing of God would be removed from his people. They, who had oppressed and trampled the poor, would themselves become poor and oppressed.

Verse 12 reminds us that God knew about every one of their offenses. There was not a single sin that was hidden from him. He knew how they were oppressing the righteous and taking bribes to pervert justice. He saw how justice was being denied to the poor while those who had money could buy their innocence.

According to verse 13, the prudent man was to keep quiet in these times. We should not understand by this that the wise man should simply sit back and let evil prevail in the land. If this were the case God would not have called Amos to speak out against the injustice. Scripture encourages the believer to stand up and defend the rights of the poor and the oppressed. Why, then, is the prudent man to be silent in such a time as this?

In verse 12 Amos told us that even the righteous were being oppressed. The whole system of justice was perverted. When a righteous man stood up against the evil system he would only encourage more wrath from corrupt officials who were unwilling to listen to the cause of righteousness. In certain cases it may be better to accept a small miscarriage of justice than to protest against a corrupt system and make matters worse. These were evil days. God's people were to rely upon him to fight the evil system. Sometimes the heart of man is so hard that he will no longer listen to reason or even to the voice of God. In times like this, the people of

God must wait upon him for justice.

Again God pleads with his people to seek good and not evil in order that they might live. It was not his desire that they should be condemned. He did not find any secret pleasure is squashing them like a young child squashing bugs. God gives them every opportunity to repent of their evil and live. He promises them his presence if they would turn to him. In verse 14, however, we see that they had driven God away by their rebellion and evil even though they believed God was still with them. Amos calls his people to return to God and his ways in the hope that God might have mercy and pardon their offenses. Their only hope was to admit their wrong and return to God with a whole heart, casting themselves wholly upon his mercy and compassion.

Verses 16 and 17 paint a prophetic picture of what would happen on the day of God's wrath. The streets would be full of wailing people. Anguish would be heard in the town squares. Farmers would mourn because there was no crop. The vine growers would wail because of the fruitless vines. Unless they repented, the Lord would pass through their midst, and the whole land would experience the judgment of God.

There are many individuals and churches in the same situation as God's people in the days of Amos. God has removed his presence from them, but they have not even noticed. The good news is that despite the fact that many of us have chased God away by our sins, he is willing to forgive. He promises to make his presence known to those who repent of their sins and seek him.

The sad reality of the matter here is that God's people don't even understand that anything is wrong in their relationship with him. They don't even know that he has removed his blessings. They have accepted their barrenness as being normal. They don't understand that God has removed his presence. Does any of this sound familiar?

In our materialistic and corrupt generation have we not fallen into the same trap? Has the enemy been successful in blinding our eyes to the absence of God? May this passage challenge us to return to the Lord and seek him. May we no longer accept the spiritual barrenness around us as normal. May we wake up to the reality that our society has driven God from our midst. May our souls cry out for him and his presence in our lives.

For Consideration:

- Examine your own spiritual life and that of your church. Is there evidence of spiritual fruitfulness?

- What do you suppose is the evidence of God's presence in our personal and church lives?

- Are spiritual dryness and barrenness normal for our personal and church lives? What in particular do you suppose holds back the pouring out of God's blessing?

For Prayer:

- Ask God to make his presence more evident in your personal and church life.

- Ask him to reveal those things that stand between you and the outpouring of his blessings.

- Ask God to forgive you for accepting fruitlessness as being normal. Ask God to equip you to more fully serve him.

7

Woe to the Religious

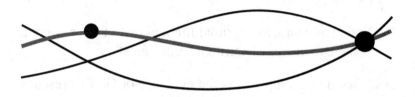

Read Amos 5:18–6:7

When the Day of Judgment comes, there will be many surprises. Perhaps the most surprising of all will be what happens to those who are dependent on their religious activities to make them right with God. In this passage, Amos speaks to those who long for the Day of the Lord. It is generally believed that the person who longs for the Day of the Lord is the person who has nothing to fear. Those who long for the Day of the Lord see themselves as being right with God and therefore wait with expectation of a heavenly reward. This passage tells us, however, that many of those who long for the Day of the Lord will be unpleasantly surprised.

Notice how these people felt about the Day of the Lord in this passage. They longed for it. The Hebrew word used here means "to lust after, covet, crave, desire, or yearn." The idea is very clear. These people are looking forward with great expectation and enthusiasm to the coming of the Lord.

Contrary to their belief, however, this day would be a day of darkness not light.

Have you ever had your expectations shattered? Maybe you had great hopes for a young child but those hopes were dashed when you heard the news that his life was snuffed out in a traffic accident. Maybe you returned home one day to see your house engulfed in flames. Never had you anticipated that you would lose everything in a few short hours. Life is full of surprises and uncertainties.

Amos gives us a few examples from his culture in verse 19. He compares the Day of the Lord to a man fleeing from a lion. As he runs with all his might, he runs straight into a bear. It is like a man who after being chased by a lion, rushes into his house and slams the door shut. With his heart pounding and out of breath, relieved that he has finally escaped, he rests his hand upon the wall only to be bitten by a poisonous snake.

Jesus also reminds us that the Day of the Lord will bring many surprises. Look at what he says in Matthew 7:22–23, "Many will say to me on that day, 'Lord, Lord, did we not prophesy in your name, and in your name drive out demons and perform many miracles?' Then I will tell them plainly, 'I never knew you. Away from me, you evildoers!'" I am sure that the individuals of whom Jesus spoke here were looking forward to the Day of the Lord like the people in Amos' day. They were more surprised than anyone to find out that their names were not written in the book of life.

Verses 21 and 22 tell us that these people who longed for the Day of the Lord were very religious people. Notice here that they are involved in the celebration of religious feasts. They participate in their religious assemblies. They bring regular burnt offerings, grain offerings, and fellowship offerings as required by the law. They, no doubt, took great pride in the fact that they were so religious. The problem, however, was that God refused to accept their offerings. In verse 21 he tells them that he despised their religious feasts and could not stand their assemblies. Their religious songs were an unwelcome noise in his ears. Why does God use such strong language here? Why does he refuse to accept the worship of these individuals? He was looking for justice and righteousness (verse 24), which, according to Amos 5:7, God's people despised and cast aside. God rejected their worship because they were guilty of oppressing the righteous and depriving the poor of justice. This was also why the Day of the Lord would be a very dark day for them.

It is important for us to understand from this that we cannot separate our worship of God from our relationships with other people. This passage clearly tells us that God refused the worship of those who are not in a right relationship with their fellow man. This is also very clear in the teaching of Jesus in the New Testament. According to this passage, then, there is no such a thing as Sunday Christianity. If we are not Christians for the entire week, we must not expect to be one on Sunday when we come to worship. Christianity must affect every part of our lives. It must impact how we work and what we read and what we do in our spare time. It must seep down into our thought life and our quiet moments alone.

In verse 25 God reminds his people of the time when they were wandering in the wilderness. He asks the question, "Did you bring me sacrifices and offerings when you were in the wilderness for forty years?" As we examine the period of wilderness wandering, when Israel moved from Egypt to the Promised Land, commentators tell us that there is really no reference to any kind of sacrifice being made from the time they left Mount Sinai until they arrived in the Land of Promise. It is quite possible that their sacrifices were put on hold for forty years. Hence God tells them in verse 25, "Even though you offered me no sacrifices in the wilderness during the forty years of wandering, yet you lifted up the shrine of your king, your idols and gods that you made for yourself." All through their wilderness wanderings they had been rebellious against God and sought other gods. Now they had repeated this error and for this, God would send them into exile beyond Damascus.

Like the people in Noah's day, these people had no concern for the future. According to chapter 6, verse 1, they had become complacent. They felt comfortable and had no worries in Zion (Jerusalem, the capital of Judah). They felt secure in Samaria (the capital of Israel). Nothing evil could happen to them; after all, they were the chosen people of God. They were the faithful givers to the work of the temple. They brought their offerings every week. What could possibly go wrong?

God speaks particularly here to the notable men of Israel who served as leaders of God's people (verse 6:1). They saw their nation as the foremost nation on the earth. They were proud of what they had done for their country. Look at their boast in verse 5:26, "Are they any better than we are? Do they have any more land than we have?" Do you see what is happening here? They are doing what each one of us has the tendency to do. They are comparing themselves to others. When placed beside other regions they felt pretty good. They saw that their prosperity was equal and, in some ways, greater than their neighbors' and so they felt that things were all right.

How often do we look at what other people are doing and measure our spirituality by what we see in others? It's easy to feel secure if we can measure up to others' level of spirituality. This is not the standard by which we must measure ourselves, however. The only true standard by which we can measure ourselves is the Word of God. This may mean that we will have to step away from the crowd. It may mean that we will have to walk alone with God. Those who measure themselves by what they see in others will always fall short of the standard that God has laid out in his word because none of us have ever attained his standard.

How does God respond to this attitude? "You put off the evil day and bring near a reign of terror," (verse 6:3). In what way were they putting off the evil day? Was it not by refusing to hear about it? Like Felix who listened to Paul preach about the judgment to come, they too said, "When I find it convenient I will send for you," (Acts 24:25). They had too many things they wanted to get out of life to listen to someone speak to them about a day of judgment. Later, after they had enjoyed a full, pleasurable life, they would listen, but for now they put it off. In so doing they quickened the beginning of the reign of terror. In other words, their unbelief and rebellion would cause God to hasten his judgment upon them.

Notice in verses 4 to 6 how these individuals had been lulled to sleep by their materialism. They slept in beds inlaid with ivory. They had nothing better to do than lounge on their fancy couches. They dined on the finest food and listened to the finest music. They drank wine by the bowl and bathed in expensive lotions. These individuals lived in the lap of luxury. Their money was all they needed. Their lives were filled with entertainment, food, and relaxation. They had reached the top. They were the envy of those around them. They were the people everyone admired.

The problem was, however, that they did not grieve over the "ruin of Joseph." To what does this phrase refer? Could this have been a reference to the prophetic word of the prophet Amos and other prophets like him who predicted that God would come in judgment upon his people? The descendants of Joseph were certainly in spiritual ruins. The notable men cared nothing about prophetic predictions. They lived for the luxuries of the moment. They refused to spoil their day by listening to predictions of coming judgment. For this reason, Amos prophesies that they would be the first to go into exile. Very soon they would lose everything they had. Their days of feasting and lounging would come to an abrupt end.

Amos is not just speaking to the people of Israel in his day; he is speaking to our materialistic, self-satisfied culture as well. We cannot read this passage without feeling that Amos is speaking to us. God's word transcends time. Human nature has not changed. This passage challenges those who are secure in themselves and their money to question their security. The Day of Judgment approaches. All our religion, wealth, and prosperity will not mean anything on that fearful day. We must make it our first priority to know for sure that we have a reservation guaranteed in heaven. We must not let the things of this world stand in the way of knowing Christ.

For Consideration:

- List some of the false securities that people cling to in our day. What do they think will get them into heaven?

- What is there in this passage that speaks directly to our own day? What were these people of Amos' day wrestling with that we are wrestling with today?

- Can we be sure that we have a place reserved for us in heaven? What gives us that assurance?

For Prayer:

- Do you know anyone like the people described in this passage? Take a moment to ask God to open up their eyes that they might see their need for a Savior.

- Ask God to reveal to you any way in which the things of this world have stood between him and you.

8
Rejoicing Over LoDebar

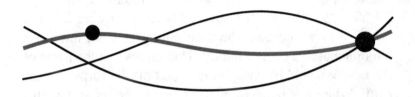

Read Amos 6:8–14

I n the last meditation we saw how the Lord warned the religious people of the land to turn away from persecuting the righteous. In verse 8 we find that it was the pride of these people that stirred up God's anger against them, for it was pride that allowed them to live luxurious lives at the expense of the poor. Pride is a horrible thing. It pushes God aside and places self on the throne. Pride was the downfall of Satan and it has been the downfall of many who claim the name of Christ in our day. Because of pride, God's people began to feel self-sufficient. They began to feel that they did not need God. Even though they took pride in their religious efforts, they forgot God. It is for this reason that God swears that he will judge his people. What follows is not pleasant but serves to accentuate the intense hatred God has for pride in the hearts of his people.

God tells his people that he will destroy Jerusalem and everything in it because it was the source of their pride (verse 8). Under the reigns of David and Solomon the city of Jerusalem had become the envy of the world. Kings came from afar to see the wealth and beauty of this great city. God had delighted to prosper them. He richly poured out his blessings and filled them with joy and prosperity. Because of their pride, however, all of this would change. Their city would be taken from them and delivered up to the surrounding nations. The rich blessings they enjoyed would be plundered. Their city would be left barren and abandoned. The pride of the whole earth would be brought down.

Verse 9 tells us that even if only ten men were left in a house, they would die. The term house does not refer to a building but to a clan or family. This means that the name of the family would be completely wiped off the surface of the earth. While this may not matter much to us in our day, this was one of the greatest fears of the Israelites. Their culture and livelihood were dependent upon their heritage. This shows us the thoroughness of God's judgment upon the land.

In verse 10 there is a scene of a relative who comes into the house to search for survivors and dispose of the dead (in this case by cremating them). If he found a survivor when he entered the house, he was to caution him about mentioning the name of the Lord. Why would the survivor be cautioned about mentioning the name of the Lord? The answer seems to be in the fact that it was the Lord who had sent this terrible calamity. Amos made this clear in verse 3:6. For fear of further offending God, they were not even to mention his name. As condemned sinners they were not even worthy of speaking the name of the Lord with their lips.

In verse 11 God describes what will happen to their houses and material possessions. In his anger against them, the Lord had given his command to smash the houses of the land to pieces. Both the large mansions and the humble huts would be destroyed in the great judgment of God.

In verses 12 and 13, Amos further explains why the

Lord was so angry with his people. This section begins with a series of questions. Each of these questions is answered negatively. Do horses run on rocky crags? Obviously not, to do so would be to risk breaking their leg. Would you ask your ox to plough a rocky crag? Not only would this be cruel, it would also be very foolish. Nothing can be planted on a rocky crag. It serves no useful purpose for which an ox would be required.

The purpose of these questions is to show God's people how foolish they were. While they had enough sense not to take their horses or oxen to a rocky crag, they did not have enough sense to remain true to the principles of justice and righteousness that God required of them. Just as they would risk the lives of their animals by taking them on to a rocky crag, so they risked their own lives by turning away from the principles of justice and righteousness.

In verse 13 God uses a play on words to further condemn the pride of his people. In the New International Version, two geographical regions are mentioned. The city of Lo Debar and the city of Karnaim were both located to the north of Israel. God reminds his people of how they had been boasting in the recent conquest of these two cities (possibly under Jeroboam II, see 2 Kings 14:28). In this conquest they had failed to give the glory to God. They became proud and boasted of these achievements as if they had been done in their own strength. What we fail to see here in the English, however, is the play on words. *Lo Debar* sounds very much like the Hebrew word "nothing." *Karnaim* is the word for "horn," a symbol of strength and power in ancient times. The King James Version translates this verse as, "Ye which rejoice in a thing of nought (*lo debar*), which say, 'Have we not taken to us horns (*karnaim*) by our own strength?'" The point is that God's people claimed that they had taken the enemies' power in their own strength, but in reality they were rejoicing over *nothing*.

Because of their pride, God was stirring up a nation that would rise against them (verse 14). This nation would oppress God's people all the way from *Lebo Hamath* (this Hebrew word means "entrance") in the extreme north to *Arabah* in the extreme south. No part of the land would escape his judgment.

What does this passage have to do with us today? Amos is writing to people who lived at a time very much like our own. In our materialistic, self-sufficient society, we too have fallen away from God. Never have things been easier or more convenient than in our day. We boast of great technological advances. We pride ourselves in being able to understand more about the human mind and the world around us than any age before us. A quick look at the state of the church, however, shows us that while we have indeed made great progress in other areas, we have taken a big step backward in spiritual matters. We no longer have any time for God. Television and entertainment have squeezed him out of our family and church lives. What does God have to say to our society as it boasts of its tremendous achievements? Verse 13 is the answer.

This passage shows us what God thinks of the pride of man. How did you get where you are today? Have you ever found yourself patting yourself on the back for the great things you have been able to achieve in life? Remember that were it not for the grace of God you would have nothing. All that you have amounts to nothing if you do not have God. May God teach you how utterly dependent upon him you actually are.

For Consideration:

• What is the challenge of this passage to our present-day materialistic, self-sufficient society?

- In what way have our achievements and advances taken our attention away from God?

- Which of these modern advances or comforts have taken you personally away from God?

- Take a moment to consider the incredible advances in technology, medicine, and science that have been made in recent years. Do you think that these advances threaten God? How much bigger than these is God?

For Prayer:

- Take a moment to confess any shortcomings this passage may have revealed to you.

- Ask God to give you the grace to put aside the distractions of this modern age and take more time with him.

- Take a moment to consider where you would be without the Lord. Thank him for the things he has saved you from.

- Thank the Lord that he is far bigger than all the science, medicine, and technology that exist in our day. Thank him for these footprints, which reveal his presence.

9

The Plumb Line

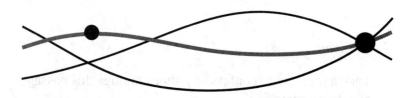

Read Amos 7:1–17

In the first part of chapter 7, Amos is given three visions. Each of these visions deals with God's judgment of his people for their sins. We will examine these visions in this meditation.

In the first of the three visions (verses 1–3), the Lord shows Amos what is going to happen to his people. Amos sees a great swarm of locusts preparing to strip the land of its vegetation. This swarm is going to come upon the land just as the second crop is about to be harvested. It is of importance to note that the people depended upon the second crop for their livelihood because the majority of the first crop went to pay taxes. Thus the locusts are coming to destroy the food source of the people. Without it, they will perish.

In chapter 6 we saw how the people had been lying in beds inlaid with ivory, dining on fatted calves and choice lambs, and drinking wine by the bowl. In their luxury, they did not give glory to God or grieve over the spiritual condition of the land. Instead they became proud and indifferent to God. There is no doubt that this is the reason for God's harsh judgment of the land. As Amos looks on in horror at what was happening in his vision, his heart cries out to God for his people. "Forgive!" he cries. "How can Jacob (representing God's people as a whole) survive, for he is so small?" Amos sees his people as they really are. He sees them as insignificant, pathetic people. This is certainly not how they saw themselves. They were confident, haughty, and believed they were a mighty nation. Amos, however, sees them from God's perspective.

Is this not a lesson our own society needs to learn? Shouldn't we realize that the greatest things of man are insignificant when contrasted to the greatness of the Sovereign God of the universe? As great as we have become through our scientific, medical, and technological advances, God still realizes our smallness. As great and as important as we think we are, our bodies are extremely fragile. We are completely dependent upon our surroundings for survival. Raise or lower the temperature just a few degrees and we perish. Change the mixture of oxygen and we perish. Any number or combination of small changes to our environment can be catastrophic. How frail we are! How utterly dependent we are upon God! How often, however, do we fail to recognize this fact and boast of our greatness just like the people of Amos' day?

Amos pleads with God for his people because he realizes their frailty. He asks God to forgive them of their sin. He recognizes how small they really are and how dependent they are upon God. In answer to this prayer, God relents. He agrees that he will not send the swarm of locusts. Isn't it amazing how the prayer of Amos stayed the hand of God? Israel was spared this horrible catastrophe because Amos prayed. Do you realize that your prayers have a very definite impact on this world? What has God accomplished through your prayers? How many people have been kept from sin or spared from its consequences because you prayed to God for them? It is good to be reminded that God listens to the prayers of his saints.

In his second vision, Amos hears God calling for a judgment of fire upon the land (verses 4–6). He sees the "fire" dry up the great deep and devour the land. What is this fire? From the context it appears that the fire is a great drought. So severe is this drought that it dries up the sea (referred to here as the great deep). Without water, proud men wither away like helpless plants. Again, Amos sees how small his nation really is (verse 5), and again he cries out for God to stop his judgment. For the second time, the Lord hears the cry of Amos and relents of the calamity he was about to send upon his people. Amos stands in the gap between sinful Israel and a Holy God. We are left only to guess what would have happened to Israel had Amos not been petitioning God on their behalf.

Could it be that because of your prayers, many sinners will be spared the flames of hell itself? Let us not grow weary in this ministry of prayer. Let us continue, like Amos, to seek God on behalf of sinners.

The third vision in this passage is the vision of a plumb line (verses 7–9). A plumb line consists of a long cord with either a stone or a piece of metal attached to the end. The line is dangled from a height to determine if a wall is straight. In his vision, Amos sees the Lord himself standing beside a wall with a plumb line in his hand. He explains to Amos that the time had come for him to set the plumb line to his people. What does this plumb line represent? Is it not the standard that God had laid out for his people in his Word? Notice that the plumb line is in the hands of the Lord. It is he who determines what is straight.

In the modern age we have many conflicting standards of measurement. We live in an age of relativism that tells us that what is wrong for one person is not wrong for another. The plumb line has become nothing more than an individual's own happiness. The day is coming, however, when God will set the plumb line among us. How can we be prepared for that day? If we want to be prepared we must measure ourselves according to the same standard that God is going to use, that is, his Word. This is his plumb line. When the Lord judges, it will be according to the standard he has laid out for us in his Word. How will you measure up?

As for Israel, she did not measure up. Like a building whose walls were crooked, Israel would have to be torn down. Her high places, where she had set up her idols, would be torn down. Her sanctuaries would be ruined. The sword of God's judgment would rise up against the house of Jeroboam because she did not meet God's righteous standard.

What Amos had to say to the people of his day was not well accepted. In fact, we have a record of the response of Amaziah, the priest of Bethel, to the words of Amos. He accuses Amos of raising a conspiracy against the very heart of Israel. He did not appreciate what Amos had to say about Israel, her sin, and the coming condemnation of the house of Jeroboam (see verse 11). Sometimes the strongest reaction to spiritual truth comes from the most religious people. The strongest reaction to the ministry of Christ came from the Pharisees who were considered to be the strictest observers of the law of God. This is what we are seeing in this passage.

Amaziah believed that something needed to be done to stop Amos from prophesying. The land "could not bear all his words." He seems to be the type of man who would only preach gentle, sweet sermons, not the sort that would rile up his people. Like many preachers of our day, his goal was only to please the people and keep them comfortable. He did not like the type of message that would confront sin and make people squirm. He was the type to overlook sin in his midst. Obviously, he must have blinded himself to the things that were going on in his day, for we have already seen how God's people had been living. They had turned their backs on God and were setting up foreign idols throughout the land. Despite this, Amaziah saw himself as being the defender of the people and their faith. Though a priest, he became an instrument of Satan to hinder the true preaching of the Word of God that condemned sin and luxurious living. It is for this reason that Amaziah calls for Amos to leave Bethel, return to his hometown and do his prophesying elsewhere (verse 12).

In verses 14 and 15, Amos tells Amaziah that he is neither a prophet nor the son of a prophet but a simple shepherd. God had called him, however, and told him to prophesy to the people of Israel. Here before us we have the well-educated Amaziah with all his polished language and liturgy opposing the rough and simple shepherd Amos. Despite his training and polish, Amaziah did not recognize the voice of God. On the other hand, Amos, the uneducated shepherd, stood firmly for the Lord and spoke in his name. While God could have used a man like Amaziah, he chose Amos.

Could it be that you are like Amaziah? Maybe you were trained in seminary and have a respectable position in your church, but like Amaziah, all these things simply stand in the way of your relationship with God. You still partake in tradition and form but have lost sight of God and the truth of his word.

The people saw Amaziah as being their defender. In God's eyes, however, he was just the opposite. He had failed his people. He had fought against God's message. For this, God would judge him. His own wife would become a prostitute in the city. The sword would kill his sons and daughters. His land would be measured up and given away. He himself would die in a foreign land, exiled from his people. Everything that Amos said came true. The world now sees who truly was the prophet of God.

The punishment for Amaziah is severe but should instruct us that God does not take lightly those—especially those in positions of spiritual leadership—who despise his word. This chapter calls us to take the plumb line of the Word of God and measure our personal and church lives accordingly. Where would you stand if you were called today to measure your life according to the standard of the Word of God? Where would your church stand? May God continually remind us of the importance of living for him according to his standard and not our own.

For Consideration:

- What is the result of the removal of the Word of God from our land and churches today?

- When you remove the Word of God, what is left to determine how we should live? What is the result of this in our society?

- Give some examples of how we have been getting away from the plumb line of God's Word.

- What do we learn here about Amos' lack of education? Was this a real hindrance to him in serving the Lord? What was the difference between Amos and Amaziah?

For Prayer:

- Pray for those in spiritual authority. Ask God to give them boldness to stand up for the principles of God's Word.

- Ask God to give you a real desire for his Word and to show you where you fall short of his standard.

- Ask the Lord to reach down in mercy upon your church and your land. Ask him for a great movement of his Holy Spirit in your midst and a great turning to God.

10
A Basket of Ripe Fruit

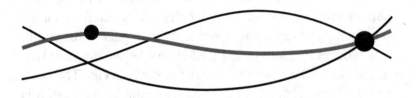

Read Amos 8:1–14

Amos had three visions in chapter 7: a vision of locusts devouring the land, a vision of a great drought, and a vision of a plumb line. Each of these visions spoke of the coming judgment of God. Here in chapter 8 the prophet has yet a fourth vision. This time he sees a basket of ripe fruit. What is the significance of this basket of ripe fruit? In verse 2 the Lord tells Amos that just as the fruit in his basket was ripe so was the time for judging. The Lord goes on to describe to his prophet what he had in store for his people. We will examine this in some detail.

What would happen to the people of God because of their sin? First, the joyous songs to God in the temple would be turned to wailing (verse 3). No longer would God's people come to the temple to celebrate his blessing and goodness, they would now come with heavy hearts. In tears they would weep and mourn because the blessing and presence of God had been removed from their midst. Their sin would cause nothing but oppression and misery.

We will return to verses 3 to 6 in a moment, but for now let's continue to paint the picture of the judgment of God against his people. The description continues in verse 8. The whole land would tremble under the terrible judgment of God. A great earthquake would cause the earth to rise like the Nile River in its flooding. It would destroy everything in its path.

Verse 9 shows us that the earth would not be the only part of creation to suffer under the heavy hand of God's judgment. The sky itself would feel the impact of his wrath. The prophet Joel tells us in Joel 2:30 that before the great Day of Judgment there would be signs in the heavens. The book of Revelation also indicates that this would be the case. It is possible that Amos is referring to the final Day of Judgment here. The possibility should not be ruled out, however, that this actually took place in the days of Amos. Commentators tell us that there were two solar eclipses during this time in Israel. Could it be that God used these eclipses to warn his people of their evil ways?

God also tells his people that the days of feasting and celebrating would soon end (verse 10). This would take place because the Lord had removed his blessing from Israel. In light of the calamity that had struck the land, God's people would be forced to mourn and wail. They would go about in sackcloth because of God's judgment upon them.

Finally, in verse 11 we see that part of the judgment of God upon the land would come in the form of a great famine. While it is quite possible that God did send a physical famine to the land, we are told here that this famine would be spiritual as the people went hungry for the Word of God. God had often spoken to his people but they had refused to listen. Now, God would no longer speak to them. The prophets would be silent. God's word would no longer be heard in the land. According to verse 12, the effects of this would be felt throughout the land. Where there was no Word, people would begin to stagger and wander around without direction. They would be like a ship tossed on the sea without a compass. They would search for the Word of Truth in their hearts but there would be no one to point them in the right direction. They would go to the priests but the priests would not be able to direct them in the path of truth because they themselves did not know it.

Could it be that we ourselves are going through a similar famine in our land? There are individuals who flounder all around us. They have been to one church after another but have not found what they have been looking for. Verse 13 gives us the picture of men and women fainting because they do not have the Word of God. How many of these people do we meet in our day? Like the people in the days of Amos, they too are tossed like a ship without a compass.

While God's people had every opportunity to hear the Word of God, they turned their backs on it and sought other gods. These gods are mentioned in verse 14. We meet the "shame of Samaria," the god of Dan, and the god of Beersheba. God was not blind to what his people were doing. By refusing the God of their fathers they had sealed their eternal fate. They would perish and never rise again.

Now, let's return to verse 4 to discover why the anger of God was so real against his people. First, God has always held the needy close to his heart. Here in verse 4, however, we see that God's people had been oppressing the needy. In fact, verse 4 tells us that they "swallowed up" (NKJV) the poor. That is to say, they destroyed them like a lion devouring its prey. By mistreating the poor of the land, they had offended the God who made them in his image.

Second, we see in verse 5 that God's people also showed contempt for God in how they despised his holy days. "When will the New Moon celebrations be over so we can sell our grain," they would say. "When will the Sabbath day be over so we can take our wheat to market," they asked each other. We see here a people who viewed these holy days as an interruption of business. It was a real bother for them to have to go to the temple and observe the religious laws. The law of God was not a delight to them because they were not in a right relationship with him. He was not pleased with half-hearted obedience. It infuriated him that his people would worship their material possessions and their work above him.

Third, God's people were guilty of resorting to dishonesty and injustice to promote their own ends. They would skimp on their measurements, boost their prices, and cheat customers by using dishonest scales. They would buy the poor and use them as slaves to promote their own interests. When the needy could not pay their bills, they would be sold as slaves so that their creditors could buy a new pair of sandals. When God's people put their wheat in bags for their customers they would put the sweepings off the floor into the bag to make it heavier and cheat the customer (verse 6).

God saw everything they had done and swore by the Pride of Jacob that he would not forget their evil dealings. What is the Pride of Jacob? Jacob is a reference to the people of God. What is the pride of the people of God? Is it not God himself? God swears by himself that he would deal with the sins of his people.

The sins of God's people are the same sins we have to deal with in our society. They worshipped the god of materialism. They lived in a time of great prosperity. It was this prosperity, however, that drew them away from God. Soon they began to seek after wealth and prestige rather than righteousness. The god of materialism gripped them. It led to dishonesty, greed, complacency, injustice, pride, and religious apathy. They became comfortable and no longer saw any need for God. Their faith became a hindrance to their progress in business. All that mattered was the present moment and how they could gain more wealth and comfort for themselves. Amos speaks very clearly of God's hatred of these sins. He gives us a clear example of what happens to those who worship the god of materialism. May we listen and escape the clutches of this horrible enemy.

For Consideration:

- What does this section of Scripture teach us about the evils of materialism?

- To what extent do you feel that the god of materialism has influenced the church in our society? What about you personally?

- Why is this god so attractive?

- Could it be said that our society is ripe for the judgment of God?

For Prayer:

- Ask the Lord to deliver you from the temptations of our materialistic society.

- Take a moment to pray for the society in which you are living. This section of Scripture has some very stern warnings against materialism. Ask the Lord to open the eyes of those who have been trapped by this god so that they might see their need of a Savior.

- Thank the Lord for his incredible patience in dealing with us even though we have not always been faithful to him.

11

Refined and Purified

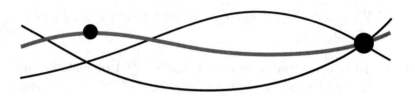

Read Amos 9:1–15

There are times when simply speaking to someone isn't enough to change their behavior. Any parent knows that from time to time their children need to be physically disciplined. This is what is happening in the final section of the book of Amos. God has spoken through his prophet throughout this book but his people have refused to listen. God must now punish his people in order to get them to change their ways. He must refine them in order to remove sin from their midst.

The passage begins with Amos seeing a vision of the Lord standing by the altar. The altar in the temple was where sins were atoned for. It is not without reason that the Lord stands here, for from the very place where sins could be forgiven, judgment is handed out. Israel had spurned God's offer of forgiveness. They had made a mockery of the altar. They had offered their sacrifices with a heart that was not in tune with God. Now they would be condemned for their sin from the very place that could have fostered God's mercy.

Amos then hears the Lord calling for the tops of the temple pillars to be struck so that they might come crashing down upon the people in the temple. It is important that we realize that the people are still in the temple as God calls for its destruction. They had not stopped being religious. They had, however, stopped seeking God. The two do not necessarily go together. Thus judgment begins in the temple with those who claimed to be living in communion with God. The reference to the shaking of the thresholds and the falling pillars resembles the language of the earthquake Amos prophesied of in the first chapter. Those who escaped being crushed by the collapsing temple would be murdered by the sword. No one would escape the terrible judgment of God upon the land.

The Lord emphasizes this point in the next few verses. If they were to dig down into the depths of the earth, the hand of the Lord would reach down and take them up. If they were to climb up to the heavens, God would reach up and pull them down. If they were to hide themselves on Mount Carmel, God would hunt them down. If they tried to go to the bottom of the sea, God would command a sea serpent to find them and devour them. Even if their enemies were to drive them from the land, God would send a sword to slay them. God's eyes were fixed upon them. There was no place they could hide from his all-seeing eyes. Their destiny was sealed.

What a horrible situation that would be! They had not made an enemy of a mere man; they had become enemies with God himself. This was the God whose very touch melted the earth, the God whose presence caused the earth to shake and rise up like the flooding Nile. He was the one who built in the heavens or on the earth as he wished. He was the one who poured water in the form of rain upon the earth. This is the God the Israelites had offended by their constant refusal to listen to his word.

In verse 7 God reminds his people that while he had

brought his people out of the land of Egypt during the days of Moses, he had also done the same thing for other nations as well. He reminds his people that he had brought the Philistines from the region of Caphtor and the Syrians from Kir. So now that they were no longer living for the Lord, what was it that distinguished them from everyone else? Why did they expect that they would be sheltered from the judgment of God when they no longer served him?

God's wrathful eyes were on the sinful kingdom of Israel, yet they would not be completely destroyed. As a nation they would be shaken like grain in a sieve to separate out the chaff and stones. Just as the grain would fall into the bag while the chaff and stones would remain in the sieve, so the righteous would be protected while the sinners were punished. Not a single pebble would fall into the bag of good grain, nor would a single sinner be left uncondemned by God.

Notice in verse 10 how the people did not expect that they would be judged for their sins. Many were saying, "Disaster will not overtake or meet us." To their surprise they *were* judged. No one escaped the wrath of God. What a terrible day this was when God lashed out upon his own people and condemned them for their sin!

The hand of the Lord was very heavy upon his people. There was, however, a purpose in this discipline. God's purpose was to restore them to fellowship with him. While they faced a very hash sentence for of their sin, God did not abandon them entirely.

In fact, verse 11 tells us that the day would come when God would restore David's fallen tent. This tent represented the nation of Israel that had been broken under the stern judgment of God. It is also very likely that this is a reference to the temple that was destroyed by the enemy when Jerusalem was invaded. If this is the case, then it represents the ability to truly worship God, which means that God would restore a right heart in his people so that he would accept their worship.

It is a promise that the day would come when the broken pieces would be put back together and when the ruins would be rebuilt. This did indeed take place under the ministry of Ezra and Nehemiah, but we should also expect an even greater fulfilment in the days to come.

Verse 12 tells us that the day would come when Israel would possess the remnants of Edom. They would also possess the Gentiles who were called by the Lord's name. This means that salvation and the knowledge of God would come through Israel and reach to the far corners of the earth. People from every tribe and nation would bow the knee to the God of Israel. We ourselves are the ultimate fulfilment of this prophecy.

While his people had turned their backs on him, God did not completely abandon them. He still had a purpose for them. We need to be mindful of this and thank the Lord for the purposes he has for our lives. We should thank him that he will not abandon us and will complete the work that he began in us.

Verse 13 goes on to prophesy days of great prosperity for God's people. Amos tells his people that in those days, the ploughman would overtake the reaper, and the one who tread the grapes would overtake the one who was planting the grapes. The harvest would be so bountiful that they would hardly have time to finish harvesting their crops before the ploughman came to sow the second crop. The grapevines would be so plentiful that the juice would drip from the vines and flow down the mountainside to the valleys below. The people of Israel, who had been taken by force from their nation, would be brought back to the land God had promised their fathers. They would again plant vineyards and gardens and harvest crops. The nation of Israel would be planted in her own land never to be uprooted again.

What does this have to do with you and me today? First, we need to respond to the warning this passage gives to the church of our day. The followers of Christ will not be spared from the judgment of God if they refuse to listen and obey his word. Second, the nation of Israel was living at a time when things were going relatively well for them. They were enjoying a time of prosperity in the land, but God took it all from them because these things led them away from him. God still loved them and had a wonderful plan for their future, but in order for that plan to be accomplished they needed to be refined and purified. We too need to be refined of our materialistic lusts in order that we might more truly love God. Third, they had taken the altar of God for granted. They came to the altar with no real intention of dealing with their sins. God saw through their hypocrisy and judged them for who they really were. If we learn anything at all from this passage, it should be that we must take the worship of God seriously. God despises hypocrisy. We must learn from the mistakes of the Israelites and flee from this wretched sin.

It is a good reminder for us that the God who blesses can also take blessing away from us. He will not hesitate to do this if a blessing stands in the way of a deeper relationship with him. His desire is for us. He will do whatever is necessary to keep our hearts fixed on him. How we need to thank him for this type of undeserved love!

For Consideration:

- In what ways do we take the Lord for granted today? Is there a sense in which we too feel secure because of our religious lifestyle?

- What do you think would happen to the churches of our day if God were to send a general persecution?

- Is there anything that stands between you and God today? What is it? What do you need to do about it?

- Examine your own life. Are there areas of hypocrisy that you too need to deal with?

- What do we learn from this passage about the depth of God's love for his people?

- What is the purpose of the discipline of God?

For Prayer:

- Ask the Lord to reveal areas of false security in your own life.

- Thank God that you can be assured of his love even in the midst of his discipline.

- Thank the Lord for the tremendous patience he has with us in our shortcomings.

- Ask the Lord to release his people from the love of the things of this world so that they can experience the greater joy of a deep relationship with him. Pray also for yourself in this matter.

Obadiah

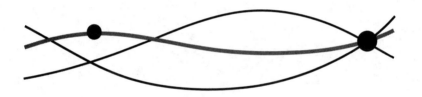

12

A Vision about Edom

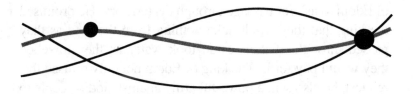

Read Obadiah 1a

Before examining the prophecy of Obadiah in detail there are a few things we should understand. Verse 1 tells us that this is the vision of a prophet named Obadiah. The name Obadiah was familiar enough in Old Testament times, but we simply do not know the identity of this particular man. No mention is made of his hometown or of his family. We must content ourselves with not knowing anymore about him than his name, which means "servant or worshipper of Yahweh." The fact that this prophet has mentioned no father or mother nor any hometown has led some to believe that Obadiah is simply a pen name for a person who prefers to remain anonymous. He simply calls himself "a servant of the Lord."

This book is a prophecy about the Edomites. Who are the Edomites? The answer can be found in Genesis 36:9, "This is the account of Esau the father of the Edomites in the hill country of Seir." Thus the Edomites were the descendants of

Esau, the brother of Jacob. We know that Jacob stole Esau's birthright and blessing. According to Genesis 27:41, Esau swore that he would kill Jacob for it after his father died. This hatred between brothers was passed on to the next generations. The prophet Ezekiel even speaks about this bitterness between Edom and the Israelites in Ezekiel 35:5. He accuses them of harboring an ancient hostility against Israel. This hostility is visible throughout the Old Testament.

For instance, when Moses was leading the children of Israel through the wilderness, he sent messengers to the king of Edom to ask for passage through his territory. He promised the king that they would take nothing from the land as they passed through. If their cattle took water as they travelled they would pay for it. The king of Edom not only refused this request, he also sent a powerful army against God's people to drive them away from his land.

We also have several occasions in the Old Testament when the Edomites joined with other forces to attack Israel (2 Chronicles 20:1–2; 21:8–10). There are also several occasions when Israel invaded the territory of Edom (2 Chronicles 25:11–12; 2 Samuel 8:13–14).

Ezekiel records Edom's hatred of Israel in Ezekiel 35:12, "Then you will know that I the Lord have heard all the contemptible things you have said against the mountains of Israel. You said, 'They have been laid waste and have been given over to us to devour.'" A little later in this same chapter of Ezekiel we read how Edom rejoiced at the downfall of the nation of Israel. This is very graphically presented to us in Psalm 137:7–8. As the children of Israel who were in exile in Babylon were reflecting upon what had happened to them, they cried out to God concerning the Edomites, "Remember, O Lord, what the Edomites did on the day Jerusalem fell. 'Tear it down,' they cried, 'tear it down to its foundations!'"

These various examples demonstrate something of the

intensity of hatred between the Edomites and the Israelites. It all began as a disagreement between two brothers. It was passed down through the generations and each generation carried this sin with them.

While this prophecy is against the Edomites, it forms part of the Old Testament for several very important reasons.

First, this book reminds us that God does not turn a blind eye to the injustice done to his children. The prophet Zechariah tells us that whoever touches God's children, touches the "apple of his eye" (verse 2:8). Edom was guilty of touching God's people and therefore God would call them to account for what they had done. Even though Israel was far from perfect in God's eyes and Scripture tells us that she had fallen short of his standard, God still held Edom accountable for the things she said and did against them. This should serve as a warning to us today. How often have we been guilty of saying negative things about God's children? God is more willing to accept us as his children than we are to accept each other as brothers and sisters, but he will not close his eyes to the injustices done to his children. The book of Obadiah is the story of the grace of God as he reaches out to his rebellious children. It is a reminder for us that God loves us despite our shortcomings. Our sins will not cause him to forsake us.

This book not only serves to remind us that God is aware of the injustices done to his children, it is also meant to be an encouragement to God's people in times of confusion. When the Israelites were defeated, they very likely replayed the image of the Edomites, standing on the sidelines, encouraging the conquest of Jerusalem (verse 12). There must have been many questions going through their minds at this time. Had God abandoned them? Did God still love them? Was God being just?

If we are honest with ourselves we would admit that we have all had moments of questioning like this. This book should bring hope to us just as it did to the Israelites. It is a book in which God speaks to those who have oppressed his people and in which he reminds his people that he will help them deal with their situation. He has not forsaken them. He loves them enough to punish their oppressors. He promises to bring them justice.

Finally, this book teaches us that God will hold everyone accountable for his or her actions. God held the Edomites accountable for what they had done to his people even though they had not been given the standard of his Word. The fact that they never believed in him made no difference either. All nations are accountable to God and will one day have to answer to him.

Countless souls remain in darkness, but they will one day have to stand before the God of Abraham, Isaac, and Jacob and give an account of their lives. God has challenged us to take the message of salvation to these individuals. The book of Obadiah is a reminder to us that we must do our part in letting the world know that there is a Savior. May God help us to be faithful witnesses.

For Consideration:

- Have you ever harbored an ancient hostility against another person? Like Edom and Jacob, have you been guilty of passing on your hostilities to others?

- If God knows about the injustices we suffer, why do you suppose he allows them to happen?

- What comfort do you receive from the fact that while you have not always been faithful to him, God is still watching over you?

- What warning do you see in this passage regarding how we need to treat the children of God?

For Prayer:

- Thank God that he is aware of your pain and will ultimately use it for your good.

- If you have been guilty of holding a grudge or speaking wrongly about another person, ask the Lord for forgiveness. What would the Lord have you do to make this situation right?

- Take a moment to pray for a particular missionary who is bringing the Word of God to people who have not had the opportunity to hear the message of the gospel.

13

Broken Pride

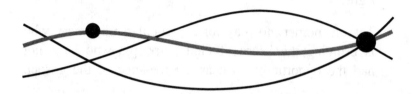

Read Obadiah 1b–9

s this prophecy begins, a special messenger is sent
to the nations of the world, calling them to do battle
with Edom. We are not given the identity of this
messenger, but it is not important.

Verse 2 then tells us that God intended to make the nation
of Edom small. The word *small* here refers to their influence
rather than size. Edom had always been geographically
small, but they had always had an influence in the political
and economic climates of the ancient Near East. Isaiah
describes them as a very rich and proud people: "Who is
this coming from Edom, from Bozrah, with his garments
stained crimson? Who is this, robed in splendor, striding
forward in the greatness of his strength? 'It is I, speaking in
righteousness, mighty to save'"(verse 63:1).

From Ezekiel 35:12 we learn that Edom was happy to
see the downfall of Israel. They said, "They have been laid
waste and have been given over to us to devour." From this

we understand that they delighted in the accumulation of possessions for themselves, for Israel's collapse meant an increase in material wealth. It is plain that their possessions gave them a sense of security. They were proud and self-sufficient. The day was coming, however, when these possessions would be taken from them, and they would become an insignificant nation.

Verse 3 tells us that the pride of their hearts had deceived them. They felt secure in their wealth and prosperity and their geographical location had always protected them from invaders. They were located on a high plain rising up four thousand feet above the sea. Commentators tell us that the plain rose up in the south to 5,700 feet. In the west, deep gorges blocked access to their borders. Approaching from the east one had to cross a great desert. In the north, deep canyons protected their cities. Edom was also defended by a series of strategically placed fortresses. This gave Edom a sense of invincibility.

Because of her situation, Edom boasted, "Who can bring us down to the ground?" (verse 3). She was confident in herself. She believed she did not need God. It is hard to read this and not be reminded of our own materialistic society. We have become like Edom. We are confident in our possessions and abilities. Never before in the history of humanity have there been such incredible advances in technology and science. We understand more about how this world works than any age before us. We are able to heal diseases thought to be incurable. Life expectancy has increased substantially. Modern conveniences have simplified daily life. We clone animals. We send satellites into space. With all these advances, however, comes a turning away from God. We no longer need him because we have mastered our world. We are able to care for ourselves. Like Edom, we even mock those who seek after God. Could the words of this prophecy be applied to our nation as well?

Notice in verse 4 what God says to those living in this false security. He reminds them that though they have made their nest in the stars and soar in the heights like a great eagle, they will be brought down. They felt that nothing could touch them, but God would prove them wrong. Such pride is a horrible thing. It places man on God's rightful throne. God does not take this lightly. Proverbs 16:18 warns us that pride always leads to destruction, "Pride goes before destruction, a haughty spirit before a fall."

What God promises will happen to Edom will happen to all who arrogantly assume that they can live without God. This is a warning we cannot afford to miss. While we boast of our great achievements, we fail to realize that our very breath comes from God. How easy it would be for him to wipe out everything the modern world has achieved. Without his constant sustaining power, we can do nothing.

In verses 5 to 7 we see the extent of the punishment that awaited Edom. God reminds Edom that if thieves came to steal from them they would only take what they wanted and leave the rest. If grape pickers came to pick grapes they would pick the best and leave a few on the vine. This, however, would not be how God would work. A greater disaster awaited Edom. Unlike the thief or the grape picker, God would leave nothing. Their destruction would be complete. Their nation would be ransacked. The treasures they loved so dearly would be pillaged. They would have nothing left.

Verse 7 tells us that they would be forced to the border by their allies. Their very own friends would turn against them and deceive them. Those in whom they relied and trusted would overpower them. Those who ate bread with them would set a trap for them. All of this would happen to them when they least expected it. They would be devastated.

What a horrible thing it is when a friend turns his back on us! Former friends are often the most vicious enemies. I cannot help but be reminded of what Jesus went through for us. He bore the punishment of our sin upon his shoulders. He was ransacked and pillaged for us. His very own friend betrayed him. The one he ate bread with set a trap for him. He willingly endured this for you and me. He paid the penalty for our sins so that we could be set free. Was Jesus thinking about these verses when he offered the bread to Judas as he sat with his disciples during the Last Supper?

According to several Biblical passages, Edom prided herself in her wise men. Eliphaz the Temanite was one of the friends who came to see Job in his time of trial (Job 2:11). Teman was a city in the region of Edom. Eliphaz was an Edomite who came to share his wisdom with Job concerning the reason for his trials. Jeremiah, the prophet, was also aware of the wisdom for which the Edomites were renowned. "Concerning Edom: This is what the LORD Almighty says: 'Is there no longer wisdom in Teman? Has counsel perished from the prudent? Has their wisdom decayed?'" (Jeremiah 49:7).

The day was coming, however, when the great wisdom of Edom would come to nothing. Their wise men, for which they were renowned, would be destroyed. Wisdom would be cut off from Edom.

Verse 9 tells us that the warriors of Teman would be terrified. These fighting men would melt like wax in the midst of the fire of God's judgment. The whole country would be cut down. There would be a great slaughter on the mountains of Esau.

Once again, we see in this section that Edom had become proud and self-sufficient. They boasted that they were invincible, that nobody could take them down. They laughed at the demise of God's people and turned their back on God. God would bring them down for this. Their great wealth and wisdom would be destroyed. Their friends would turn their backs upon them and set a trap for them. They would be left with nothing.

We desperately need to listen to the warning of this

passage. In our self-sufficient, materialistic society we often feel that we no longer need God. Even in our personal lives we act as though we can do everything on our own. We have been led to believe that there are no diseases that we cannot cure, no problems we cannot solve. Every so often we need to be reminded of the fragile nature of life and the smallness of man. God laughs at our advances in technology and medicine. He shakes his head at our arrogant attempts to master the universe. With one blow he could end it all. With one word from his lips everything we have worked for could go up in smoke. Every breath we breathe, every beat of our heart comes from him. Without him we can do nothing.

For Consideration:

- How often have you been guilty of believing that you are in control of your own destiny? Why is it so hard for us to recognize our total dependence on God?

- Where would you be today if God had not reached out and saved you?

- What does this passage teach us about pride? What will happen to those who are proud?

- What do we learn about our need for God's direction, empowerment, and wisdom in our service for him?

For Prayer:

- Ask the Lord to help you recognize your need for him. Ask him to forgive you for the times you have failed to recognize and rely upon his enabling.

- Take a moment to pray for our materialistic society. Ask God to remind us of our need for him.

- Ask God to open your mind to your need for him and his guidance each and every day. Ask him to give you the grace to seek him in all things.

14

The Progression of Sin

Read Obadiah 10–14

In the last meditation we saw the pride of the inhabitants of Edom. They believed that they were invincible. Because they believed that nothing could happen to them, Edom took some very big risks. In this section we see what she did to the children of Israel.

God accuses the Edomites of doing violence to his people. God was aware of what had happened to his children. He had not turned a blind eye to the injustice that was being done to them. Though Israel deserved God's punishment, he still cared for them as his children. He would punish Edom for the violence they had done to Israel and Judah. As a nation, Edom would be put to shame for their crimes. They would cease to exist because of what they had done to God's people. What follows is a description of this violence.

First, when the enemy attacked the city of Jerusalem, the Edomites stood at a distance and watched it take place. Like a group of children at a fight in a schoolyard, they cheered the enemy as he pulverized the children of God. This was where it all began.

How often have we stood aloof, secretly delighting in the sin around us? Consider for a moment the sin we see on television. How often do we simply sit back and watch violence and immorality? We ease our conscience by assuring ourselves that we would never act this way, yet we still enjoy watching the sins of others. In this, we allow Satan to gain a foothold in our lives and the lives of our children. Our children are being bombarded with evil through the media but we do nothing about it. We have become desensitized to sin. We have become cold and indifferent to evil. This is exactly where Satan wants us. If he can get us to this point, he can easily move us to take the next step on the road to sin.

Second, when the Assyrians conquered Israel, Edom wanted a piece of the pie. She saw a chance for her own advancement. She wasn't responsible for what had taken place. What had happened had happened, and there was nothing that would change the situation. So as the trophies of war were being divided, Edom got into the act. She wanted her share. The problem was that these goods were stolen goods. By sharing in the profits, Edom offended God, for to share in the spoils is to participate in the battle.

There is an important lesson here for us. God calls us to flee from all appearances of evil. We may think that profiting from other people's sin is not as bad as actually committing the sin. We may be lulled into believing that we can manipulate other's evil for our good without incurring God's wrath. This, however, is a grave mistake, for to profit from others' sin is to enjoy the proceeds of sin and is actually the second step on the road to sin. This is exactly where Satan wants to take us.

Third, when Edom saw Israel humbled, she rejoiced and boasted in her own good fortune. She felt that she was better than Israel because God had not judged her in this way. She rejoiced in the day of Israel's distress.

Is there not a tendency in each of us to rejoice in the fall of others? Maybe it's a coworker who failed where you succeeded or a sister who never found a husband. This tendency is not of God. The trouble of a coworker or family member ought to stir up feelings of compassion and love. It ought to stir us to humble ourselves and reach out to them in their need. Notice here that the third step on the road to sin is to enjoy the misfortune of another.

Have you ever watched people wander in their relationship with the Lord? Have you noticed how they always come to the point in their relationship with other believers when they enjoy others misfortunes? Wandering believers always need to justify their sin. The way they do so is to become bitter with other Christians. They criticize them and their ways. They find fault with their church and the believers around them. They see themselves as having a better way. When you see these attitudes, beware. Pride comes before the fall. This is the road to sin.

It is important that we do not miss the progression in this passage. We have seen first of all, that the Edomites stood aloof while others did the damage. Then she took a small step forward and began to share in the spoils. In the last verse we saw that her attitude began to change toward her brother and she began looking down on him and becoming critical of him. This eventually led to rejoicing in his downfall. The whole thing begins to snowball. Finally, in verse 13 we read that Edom boldly marches through the gates of the city to seize Israel's wealth. Her hostility is now quite open. She has courted sinful attitudes towards Israel and the fruit is now seen in her actions.

The progression from standing aloof to seizing wealth is very subtle. We need desperately to nip these attitudes in the bud before they take over our lives. No one starts by seizing wealth. It all starts by standing aloof and watching someone else do it. Gradually, like getting into a hot bath, we grow accustomed to hostile feelings. Eventually they overtake us. The enemy works ever so slowly. His tactic is to desensitize us to sin and evil. Like he did in the Garden of Eden, he leads us to question what God says. Eventually, we fall into his trap and sin is inevitable.

Notice where all of this ultimately leads the Edomites. While in verse 10 they stood aloof watching others pulverize the people of God, now they wait at the crossroads to murder the escaping fugitives. What profit did this bring them? Apart from a good standing with the enemy, the action of cutting down the escaping fugitives profited them nothing. They are no longer concerned about profit. Their intent is to persecute the people of God. The enemy has conquered their hearts and they are now motivated by hatred of God and his people. They cut down God's people without mercy. They have no compassion upon those fleeing the devastation of Jerusalem. They punch them while they are down. They take advantage of them in their weakened condition. In so doing, they seal their judgment.

The big lesson for us is to see the progression of sin in the life of Edom. It starts very innocently but soon mushrooms into something catastrophic. Satan will never be happy with just a little corner of our hearts. If we give him a foothold in our lives, he will not be content until he has taken everything. We cannot afford to allow him even the smallest corner of our lives.

Maybe you have seen this progression in the life of a friend or loved one. Maybe you are experiencing it in your own life. May God help you deal with your sin before it takes complete control.

For Consideration:

- Can you think of a personal example in your own life of this progression of sin?

- What are some of the ways in which Satan seeks to desensitize us to sin and evil today?

- What are some areas in your own life where you find yourself being tempted? What do you need to do before these small areas become very big issues in your life?

- What does this passage teach us about small sins?

For Prayer:

- Have you fallen into the trap of Satan and been drawn away from the Lord like Edom? Ask God for forgiveness.

- Take a moment to pray that the Lord would cause your wandering loved one or friend to return to him and realize the tactic of Satan in seeking to draw him away from the Lord.

- Ask the Lord to show you those areas in your life that need to be cleansed.

15
Deliverance for God's People

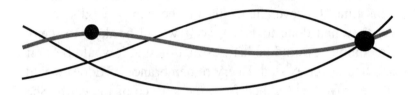

Read Obadiah 15–21

Edom has been accused of horrible crimes against the people of God. In their pride, they felt that they were secure and protected from their enemies. What they did not realize, however, was that no defense would protect them from the God of Israel. He would shatter all opposition and crash through their fortified walls to bring justice for what they had done to his people.

This section begins with the warning, "The Day of the Lord is near." Edom is not the only one who will have to give an account for her rejection of the Lord and her crimes against his people. One day all nations will stand before the Lord Jesus. On that day, they will bow the knee and recognize him as Lord. For many, however, it will be too late. What is true for the nations is also true for individuals. The Day of Judgment is coming. We do not know when it will be but we can be assured that it will come.

What is God's final word to Edom as her judge? "As you have done, it will be done to you." They had determined their own sentence. God would simply return on their heads what they had done to others, an eye for an eye, a tooth for a tooth.

Verse 16 tells us that just as Edom drank on God's holy hill, so the nations who destroyed her would drink. What had Edom drunk? Had she not drunk the cup of violence towards Israel? Did she not lift her cup in rejoicing and celebration over the defeat of God's people? Did she not revel in her victory over Israel and belittle God's people in their time of trouble? The day was coming when they would drink again. This time, however, it would be the cup of God's wrath. As they had done to Israel, so it would be done to them. So complete would be her destruction that it would be as if she had never existed. Every remembrance of Edom would be destroyed and wiped from the surface of the earth. She would be remembered no more.

At this time, the people of God were in exile. The time was coming, however, when God would deliver Israel from captivity. In verse 17, Obadiah says that God would do two things for his people. First, he would make them holy. Holiness here refers to being separated out from the rest of the nations to be pure for God. While the enemy intended to do evil to God's people, God had used their trial to refine them and draw them closer to him. The day was coming when Israel would see a fresh work of grace in their midst. God would move among them in revival power. Second, God's people would be set free from their foreign prison and return to the land God had promised to them as an inheritance. Notice the difference between the trial of Israel in verse 17 and that of Edom in verse 16. Edom's trial was final. It would be as though she had never been. As for God's people, however, their trial served to refine them and draw them back to God. God would not abandon his people forever.

In verse 18 we read that God would empower his people to render justice to Edom. Allusion is made here to the rivalry between Jacob and Esau. Jacob, according to verse 18, would become a fire. He would consume Edom and leave nothing but stubble. Esau would be completely wiped out. There would be no survivors. Once again we see that their judgment was final.

How desperately we need to be sure where we stand! There is judgment to come. For some it will be like Edom. It will be a final judgment. Once the sentence is passed, there will be no changing it.

In verses 19 and 20 a reallocation of territory is described. Edom would lose the land in which they boasted, and it would be given to others. Verse 19 tells us that the people of the Negev would inhabit the mountains of Esau. The Hebrew word here is *negeb* which can mean "south." This accounts for the KJV translation. The region of the Negev is located to the south of Judah. It was allotted to the tribe of Simeon. The idea here is that the people of God would be given the land of Esau.

The Philistines lived along the coast of Palestine. They were a constant threat to the people of God. We read in 1 Samuel 13:5–6 how the Philistines oppressed God's people and drove them up into the mountains. The day was coming when the Israelites would come down from the mountains and take the territory of the Philistines who had oppressed them. Those coming down out of the foothills would again possess the territories of Ephraim and Samaria, the capital of Israel. Benjamin would possess the region of Gilead. God would return his people to their land and re-establish them there.

Verse 20 tells us that the Israelites would possess the land from the region of Zarephath to the towns of the Negev. We have already seen that Negev was in the south of Judah. Zarephath was located in the extreme north in the area of Tyre and Sidon. The exiles would one day return and repossess this land all the way from Zarephath in the north to the region of the Negev in the south. What a promise this was for God's rebellious people! They had lost their territory because of sin. But God, in his grace, would restore it to them.

How much territory have we lost as a church today? Have we lost our influence in the community? On Cape Breton Island, where I live, there are whole communities plunged into darkness that at one time experienced revival. Who is to blame but ourselves? We have not always stood up for the truth. We have allowed sin to enter without dealing with it. We have lost much territory. God promises Israel that he would restore the territory they had lost. To do this he would begin by restoring holiness in the land. When they were again restored to a right relationship with God they would regain the territory they had lost. We must learn from this that nothing short of a revival will restore to us the territory we have lost.

From verse 21 we learn that deliverers would go up to Mount Zion, a reference to the city of Jerusalem. God would send deliverers from Jerusalem to govern this vast territory. Special mention is made here of the fact that Israel would govern the region of Edom and the mountains of Esau. The whole kingdom would be the Lord's. He would return order to it through these deliverers.

We have in this small book real encouragement for those who are struggling. This book challenges us to look to a sovereign God and realize that he really is in control. The first few paragraphs of this book paint a picture of God's people in trouble and defeat. They are oppressed and beaten, but God has not abandoned them. The time of their victory is coming. Through their difficulties they are drawn closer to God and shown his power over evil. Their enemies are handed over to them. While the punishment of God's people was only temporary, the punishment of their enemies was for eternity.

Pride had been the downfall of Edom. In their pride they felt that they did not need God. Because of this, they were destroyed. Edom's destruction was so complete that the memory of them is all but erased from the earth. They felt that nothing could happen to them. How wrong they were! The eagles of Teman were never to fly again. From her lofty height she was brought down to the ground. How our society needs to hear this message today! Even as individuals, we desperately need to recognize our need for God.

Don't let pride destroy you.

For Consideration:

- What encouragement do you take from this passage for your troubles and trials?

- Obadiah tells us that it will be done to us even as we have done to others. Is there a particular sin that you need to make right with a brother or sister?

- What territory needs to be repossessed for the Lord today? Is there a promise for us in this chapter?

For Prayer:

- Take a moment to thank the Lord that he does promise victory for those who belong to him.

- Do you know someone who, like Edom, has turned their back on God and is living in pride and rebellion against him? Take a moment and bring them to God.

- Ask God to restore to you the territory you have lost (whether this be as a church or in your personal life). Thank him for the assurance that he gives to us that he will indeed do this.

Jonah

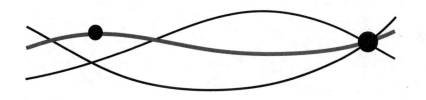

16

Headed for Tarshish

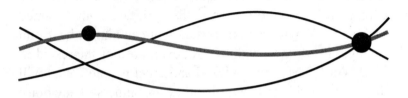

Read Jonah 1:1–3

We know very little about the prophet Jonah. 2 Kings 14:25 tells us that he came from the region of Gath Hepher in northern Israel. Apart from this, Scripture records no further details about him. His call to be a prophet came directly from God as recorded in verse 2, "Go to the great city of Nineveh, and preach against it, because its wickedness has come up before me." In order for us to fully appreciate Jonah's call, we need to understand the times in which he lived.

The city of Nineveh was a principal city in the nation of Assyria. The Assyrians were the ones who would later invade the northern kingdom of Israel and take them into captivity. From 2 Kings 14:25 we understand that Jonah prophesied during the reign of Jeroboam II. Historians tell us that Assyria was having difficulties at this time. Their military campaigns had greatly decreased and her leaders were powerless. History also indicates that Assyria passed through a great famine during this period of her history.

Could it be that God had been preparing the Assyrians for Jonah's ministry? Is this the reason why they were so responsive to the message of the prophet?

Beyond these historical details, the Bible tells us that the inhabitants of Nineveh were evil in the eyes of God (verse 2). The fact that these people were wicked would not have encouraged Jonah to preach to them. Added to these facts was the assumption of the Jews that salvation was for them alone. While God might have been concerned about the souls of these foreigners, Jonah, like his fellow Jews, had no compelling reason to preach to them. In fact, Jonah wanted nothing to do with the Ninevites. You can almost hear him saying, "Lord, the people of Nineveh are not interested in your Word. They are a wicked and cruel people. What will they do to me if I tell them that they are sinners? They don't deserve your love. Send me to my own people. They need you too."

Like many of us would do in a similar situation, Jonah decided to run away. Did he really believe he could find a place where the Lord could not find him? As a prophet he must have known that it was impossible to flee from an all-seeing and all-knowing God. So why did he run? Like Adam and Eve, Jonah felt he had to hide from the Lord. We too must make a choice. Either we obey or we run away. As for Jonah, he made his choice. He paid the price for his ticket and boarded a ship heading for Tarshish. Jonah had no idea the price he would pay for his disobedience.

We are not certain of the location of Tarshish. Many commentators believe it to be in southern Spain. If this is the case, Jonah was willing to travel approximately four thousand kilometers to hide from God. Since Nineveh would only have been approximately one thousand kilometers, obedience would have been much simpler.

There are many times when the Lord asks us to do things we do not like. The most precious things in this life, however, come at great cost. The greatest of all treasures is a personal relationship with God. This relationship does not come cheaply. It may cost us our very life. What value should we put on our relationship with God? Jonah sold his for the price of a ticket to Tarshish.

Ironically, there is not a more unhappy person on the earth than the one who is running from God. He is always running but never able to escape. The Psalmist describes this in Psalm 139:7–12 as he finds no rest when running from God.

> Where can I go from your Spirit? Where can I flee from your presence? If I go up to the heavens, you are there; if I make my bed in the depths, you are there. If I rise on the wings of the dawn, if I settle on the far side of the sea, even there your hand will guide me, your right hand will hold me fast. If I say, "Surely the darkness will hide me and the light become night around me," even the darkness will not be dark to you; the night will shine like the day, for darkness is as light to you.

Where do you stand today? Is there sin in your life that is driving you from the presence of God? Jonah found out soon enough that there is no peace outside the will of God. May God teach us this lesson today.

For Consideration:

- Take a moment to search your heart. What things take you away from the Lord?

- Have you ever had a time in your life when you ran away from the will of the Lord? What was the cost of running away from him?

- How willing are you to live in obedience? What would you be willing to sacrifice in order to be obedient to the Lord?

For Prayer:

- Do you know of someone who is running away from the Lord today? Take a moment to pray for that person.

- If there are areas in your life where you have not surrendered your will to the Lord, take a moment to seek his forgiveness. Ask him to give you victory over your sins.

17

Pursued by God

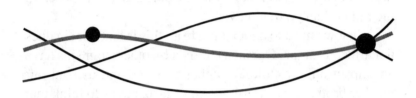

Read Jonah 1:4–7

Jonah headed for Tarshish, the opposite direction from the place God had called him. He simply could not accept the will of God for his life. The Lord could have left him alone in his disobedience and found another prophet to go to Nineveh. It was not as if Jonah was particularly qualified; in fact he was a very rebellious individual. God knew this even before he sent him, but he did not leave Jonah in his rebellion because he had a particular purpose for him.

God had a particular purpose for many of the people we find in the pages of the Old Testament. Moses tried to tell God that he was not the man to bring the Jews out of Egypt. He felt that his brother Aaron was a better man for the job. God patiently listened to Moses but nothing changed his mind. When Samuel came to anoint one of Jesse's sons, the eldest and strongest were brought out first. All of them were rejected in favor of David, the content shepherd.

In a similar way, God sovereignly placed his hand upon Jonah. God chose him to be his instrument to call the Ninevites to repentance. So he chased Jonah, sending a great wind to toss the boat in which Jonah slept. God's voice was clear. He spoke powerfully through each wave that beat against the side of the ship. Each wave cried out "Jonah, you are going the wrong way, return to the Lord." Jonah, however, rebelliously continued on his path. He did not concern himself with the impact of his sin on those around him. Rebellion had clouded his reason. Jonah had chosen to die rather than go to Nineveh.

What we need to understand from this is that our sin does not affect us alone. Our sins are seen by others; our sins have an impact on our children, unbelievers around us, and our weaker brothers. We must not be so arrogant as to think that we sin in a vacuum. The evil we do brings punishment to an entire community of people.

As the storm raged around the ship, all was utter chaos. The hardened sailors, accustomed to the storms at sea, feared for their lives. Realizing that their lives were in serious danger, they even threw their cargo overboard. Their last concern was for the profits that they were going to make on the voyage. Finally, having lost all hope in their own skills, they desperately cried out to their gods for help.

Where was Jonah throughout this ordeal? While everyone else was praying and struggling to save their lives, Jonah was down in the bottom of the ship sleeping, not praying. It is hard to imagine Jonah sleeping at a time like this. The only explanation for this is that Jonah was trying to escape from the realization of what he had done. As he slept, he no longer had to deal with what was going on around him. He no longer had to listen to the frantic cries of the sailors and be reminded of his sin.

God did not leave him alone, though. The captain of the ship, an unbeliever, found him asleep and yanked him awake. He rebuked Jonah and told him to cry out to God. This is a very powerful and prophetic image. Jonah, the chosen servant of God, was not even praying while the unbelieving captain was begging for salvation from any god that would answer him.

While this prophecy is primarily about Jonah, we need to understand that it is also a prophecy to the nation of Israel. God had specifically chosen Israel to be his people. Like Jonah, however, they had turned their backs on God. Like Jonah, they were spiritually asleep. Like Jonah, they would be driven from their homeland because of sin. Like Jonah, God would use unbelievers to awaken them from their spiritual sleep.

As Jonah slept in the bottom of the ship, the sailors, realizing that something supernatural was wrong, came to the conclusion that someone on board the ship had offended the gods. They cast lots to determine the guilty party. It was not by chance that the lot fell on Jonah, for Proverbs 16:33 tells us, "The lot is cast into the lap, but its every decision is from the LORD."

One cannot read this passage without noticing that God refuses to abandon Jonah. He had a plan for Nineveh and that plan included the prophet. It did not matter than Jonah was uninterested in God's plan. God chased him in the storm. He spoke to him through the captain. He pointed his finger at him through the sailors. God did this for his people as well. Though they had to be punished for their sin and sent into exile, God did not give up on them. He chased after them. He had a special plan for them. He loved them too much to let them go. What an encouragement this is for those of us who have loved ones who are wandering from the Lord. Though they have wandered, God has not abandoned them.

Maybe God is pursuing you today. Has he been using winds and waves of trials to get your attention? If God has been pursuing you, realize that it is because he loves you and has a special place of service for you. Don't waste another moment; submit yourself to him right now.

For Consideration:

- What are some of the ways that God used to get the attention of Jonah in this passage?

- What ways does God use to call us back to himself today?

- What do we learn from this passage about God's love for his people?

- What is the comparison between Jonah's experience and what Israel went through as a nation?

- How did God speak to Jonah on the boat? Does he speak to us in a similar way?

For Prayer:

- Thank God that he has a special purpose for your life.

- Thank God that when we run away, he does not leave us.

- Ask God to make you sensitive to the ways in which he speaks to you today.

- If you know someone who, like Jonah, is running away from the Lord, pray that the Lord God would chase after him or her until they return to him.

18

Why Did You Do It?

Read Jonah 1:8–10

Jonah did not flee very far from the presence of the Lord. God pursued him aboard the ship. The sailors, believing that the wrath of the gods was against them, wanted to know, at all costs, why the lot had fallen on Jonah. They asked him who he was, where he came from, and what his business was. Jonah was forced to recount his story.

The prophet began by telling them that he was a Hebrew who worshipped the God who created the sea and the earth. It was this God who caused the sea to swell up against them. Jonah also explained that he had been running away from this great God.

The sailors thought for a moment about what Jonah said. They looked around at the storm and then asked a very profound question, "Why did you do it?" What was going through Jonah's mind when these unbelieving sailors asked him that question? He knew that he was a prophet of God. He knew that he should not have been running from God. He knew that his life did not reflect his calling. How could he honestly answer their question?

The question of the sailors is one that had been asked many times before. Way back in the Garden of Eden, Adam and Eve enjoyed a perfect communion with their Creator. They experienced a paradise that you and I can hardly imagine. They gave it all up, however, for the price of the taste of the Tree of the Knowledge of Good and Evil. The question could very well be asked, "Why did they do it?"

More recently, the Israelites were in slavery in the land of Egypt and were being mistreated and abused. One day the Lord sent Moses to deliver them from their bondage. Through great signs and wonders, God demonstrated his love for them by destroying their enemies and delivering them from their oppressor. With great joy they left the land of their four hundred year bondage. Can you imagine that just a few weeks later these very same people would curse the God who delivered them? Again the question might be asked, "Why did they do it?"

Many years later a man by the name of Peter watched Jesus heal the sick, give sight to the blind, and raise the dead. He saw this same man spiritually transfigured on the top of a mountain. He saw nature itself obey his every command. Peter was there when Jesus took a few pieces of bread and some fish and multiplied them to feed thousands of hungry people. Can you imagine such a man denying that he ever knew the Lord when accused by a lowly servant girl? Peter, why did you do it?

The question of the sailors is very disturbing because we know that there are many times when we ourselves should be asked this very question. How could any of us ever turn our back on a God who has been so good to us? Even the apostle Paul had to admit in Romans 7:15 that "I do not understand what I do. For what I want to do I do not do, but what I hate I do." We all have to admit that there is a horrible tendency within each of us to turn our backs on God.

Why did Jonah turn his back on his God? Ultimately it was because of the terrible sin nature that lived within him just as it lives within us. That sinful nature opposes God and his ways and is one of our three great enemies. The world around us tempts us to turn our backs on the Lord God. The devil also does his best to distract us and lure us into sin. However, the world and the devil would not be able to succeed if it were not for our third great enemy, namely our sinful, human nature. It is this nature that craves the evils of the world. It is contrary to God and his purposes. It must be crucified or it will lead us away from God. Jonah followed the desires of that evil nature and fled from God. We would certainly do likewise if, even for a moment, our sinful nature were our master.

On board the ship, Jonah was forced to humble himself and admit his sin. In so doing, he took the first step back toward God. Thus we are reminded that the first step to recovery is to recognize our guilt and confess our sins to those we have offended. This may not be easy but it is a necessary step. It may be humiliating. It may cost a great deal of money, pride, or trust, but there is no other way to return to God.

Do you have sins that you need to confess? You cannot expect to grow in your relationship with God if you refuse to recognize your guilt. May God grant you the courage of Jonah. May you recognize your guilt, confess your sin, and return in the direction God has called you. Stop running from him. Make things right today.

For Consideration:

• What keeps us from confessing our sins to one another?

- What do we learn in this meditation about the sinful nature that exists in each of us? What do we need to do with this nature?

- Why did Jonah turn from his Lord and run away? Did it make sense for Jonah to try to run from the great God who created the universe? Could he really run from God at all?

- Have you ever been in Jonah's situation? What was the result of your confession of sin?

For Prayer:

- Take a moment to search your own heart. Is there anything that you need to confess to God?

- Ask God to reveal any sin in your life that he would have you confess.

- Thank the Lord that he promises forgiveness to all who will turn to him.

- Ask the Lord to give you greater victory over the sinful nature.

- Thank him that he sent his Son to give you victory over the world, the flesh, and the devil.

- Thank him that he is bigger than all of these enemies.

19
Cast into the Sea

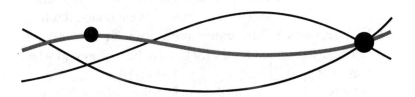

Read Jonah 1:11–16

In the last meditation, we saw how Jonah confessed his sin before the sailors. This had not been an easy thing to do. Now that they knew he was the guilty party, what would they do to him? Even more important, however, what would be the response of God?

The Bible tells us that the sea was getting rougher and rougher. What was the problem? Why wasn't it getting calmer? Had God not heard the confession of Jonah? Why hadn't anything changed? What more did God want? The sailors themselves began to wonder what to do. They now knew what was causing the storm but they were unsure of how to appease the wrath of Jonah's God. Jonah told them that the only way the anger of God would be appeased was for them to throw him overboard.

Jonah's confession was only part of the process of restoration with God. Jonah was still on a boat headed for Tarshish. He was still running from God. As long as he was living in rebellion, Jonah could not expect God's blessing. Jonah had taken the first step and admitted he was wrong. Now he needed to do something about it. As long as Jonah was on board the ship, neither he nor the crew members could be saved. The problem now was getting off a boat in the middle of the stormy sea.

Jonah had a decision to make: Was it better to live in rebellion or to die in obedience? The fact that Jonah did not simply jump off the boat may be an indication that he wasn't really sure of his choice. In so doing, Jonah forced the sailors to make the decision. His rebellion now entangled the lives and possessions of the entire crew into God's wrath. It would have been so much easier to have turned around when he was in Joppa.

Maybe as you read this meditation you understand something of what Jonah experienced. Maybe you have made a real mess of your life and hurt a lot of people. It is not always easy to make things right. Swallowing your pride and going to see someone you have offended is not easy. Like Jonah, you look out into the great sea of humiliation and uncertainty and wonder if you will ever be able to get out of the mess you've gotten yourself into. It seems much easier to simply stay where you are than to dive into the sea of uncertainty.

The sailors, not wanting to make Jonah's God angry by throwing his prophet into a watery grave, tried to row to shore. The Bible tells us that the more they rowed, the worse the storm became. The sailors needed to learn the same lesson that God was teaching Jonah, namely, that one cannot run from God and it is useless to even try.

In desperation, they finally agreed to listen to Jonah's advice and throw him overboard. Afraid of the wrath of Jonah's God, they pray in verse 14, "O Lord, please do not let us die for taking this man's life. Do not hold us accountable for killing an innocent man, for you, O Lord, have done as you pleased." Then they simply threw Jonah overboard.

Immediately, the storm ceased and the sea became calm. Notice the effect this had upon the sailors. The Bible tells us that the sailors "greatly feared the Lord." They responded by offering sacrifices and making vows to the Lord. A revival broke out on the ship as the sailors turned to the Lord. God, in his sovereignty, used the rebellion of Jonah to reach these hardened sailors.

In this passage we learn that it takes more than a simple confession to be restored to a right relationship with God. Jonah not only had to confess his sins to those whom he had offended, he also had to stop running from God. He had the courage to face the God he had offended, but that was the easy part. Getting off the boat was much more difficult.

Maybe as you read this you are still on a ship headed to Tarshish. Don't stop at confession. Like Jonah, you too will have to get off the boat of rebellion. Face the uncertainty before you and make things right. Commit yourself right now, whatever the cost, to be obedient to God and his will. While this may not always be easy, it is a necessary step toward reconciliation and renewal.

For Consideration:

• Have you ever met someone who was sorry for their sins but was either unable or unwilling to change things in their lives? Are you in any way guilty of this?

• Why do you suppose a person would confess their sin if they were unwilling to make the necessary changes?

• How important is it that we move beyond simple confession to making things right with God again?

For Prayer:

- Ask God to reveal any sin that needs to be abandoned in your life.

- Ask God to give you the strength to make the necessary changes.

- Ask him to forgive you for the times you confessed your sins but chose to remain in them.

20

In the Belly of the Fish

Read Jonah 1:17–2:10

Knowing that he had to face the Lord he had offended, Jonah permitted the sailors to cast him into the sea. Would the Lord allow him to perish in the waves? Jonah did not know. What he did know, however, was that to stay on the ship was certain death, not only for himself, but also for the crew. His life was now in the hands of the Lord.

In his sovereignty, God sent a great fish to swallow Jonah. I do not know what Jonah thought when he saw that big fish coming toward him. It is *not* very likely, however, that he saw it as his deliverance. More than likely, Jonah saw this fish as his final judgment from God.

God often uses strange means to accomplish his purpose in our lives. Sometimes the richest blessings of the Lord come disguised as horrible tragedies. These tragedies shape and remold us. In tragedy, priorities are reshuffled. We begin to see things in their proper perspective. Insignificant and petty matters lose their attraction, and spiritual matters take their proper place.

Maybe, like Jonah, you too have been cast into a sea of uncertainty and swallowed whole by a great fish of tragedy. What is your fish? What circumstance is God using to bring you into closer fellowship with Him? Instead of being bitter, why not let God accomplish his deliverance in your life?

Jonah's trial was not easy. Notice how he describes it in chapter 2 as having descended into the very "belly" or "depths" of the grave. In verses 3 to 6 Jonah tells us that the waves and breakers overwhelmed him. He sank to the depths of the earth. He felt trapped with no hope of escape. Yet when he had come to the end of himself, he cried out to the Lord. Sometimes God must use drastic means to get our attention.

God heard Jonah's cry. From the belly of the fish he came to understand an important spiritual lesson. He learned that "those who cling to idols forfeit the grace that could be theirs"(verse 8). He came to realize that there was no hope in any other god. To turn from the God of Israel was to turn one's back on the grace and mercy that he alone could give. There in the belly of the fish Jonah experienced a new understanding of God's grace.

Jonah also experienced a great personal renewal in the belly of the fish. There, in his trial, Jonah's heart overflowed into a song of joy and thanksgiving. Right then and there Jonah confessed that he had not been faithful to God and promised that he would fulfill his vows to the Lord. He promised that things would be different now. It was only at this point that God commanded the fish to spit him up on dry land. With a single word from the Lord, Jonah was delivered from his trial.

The other thing we need to see in this passage is that the Lord God was always in control of the situation that Jonah was going through. That fish was obedient to the command of the Lord. Just one word and Jonah was set free. Do you realize that the trial that you are going through is just one word away from victory? Just one word from him and everything can change. There is nothing outside of his control. Take courage in this and trust him to do what is right.

I do not know what trials you are facing today. I do know, however, that just as he did with Jonah, God can use your trial to accomplish great good. There are tremendous spiritual lessons to be learned in tragedy. I trust that, as you face your trial, you too will know God's grace and renewal.

For Consideration:

- Why do you think God uses trials and difficulties to teach us the most powerful spiritual lessons?

- Think about a recent trial that you had to face. What lessons did God teach you through that trial?

- How do we know that the Lord God was in control of Jonah's trial? What comfort does this bring you?

For Prayer:

- Thank God that he uses trials to draw us closer to him.

- If you are facing a particular trial right now, ask the Lord to help you to not miss the great lessons he wants you to learn.

- Do you know of another person who is facing a trial today? Ask the Lord to take them through this trial and draw them closer to him.

- Thank the Lord that victory is just one word away.

21

A Second Chance

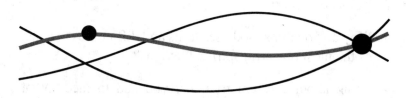

Read Jonah 3:1–2

Jonah met God in the belly of the fish. The whole experience taught him many important lessons. For three days he remained in his watery grave until the fish spit him up on dry ground. Never before had the air smelled so good. The joy of freedom flooded his heart. Praise to God filled his soul. But once again, Jonah heard the voice of the Lord: "Go to the great city of Nineveh, and proclaim to it the message I give you" (verse 2).

Do you find it incredible that the Lord would call Jonah a second time? Why would God give him a second chance when he had failed so miserably the first time? If Jonah had been an ambassador for any earthly king he would not have been given such an opportunity. He probably would have been executed. Here, though, we discover that God is a ruler who gives second chances.

Unlike men, God is willing to forgive and wipe the slate clean. When God forgives, he treats us as though we had never sinned. The prophet Micah tells us,

Who is a God like you, who pardons sin and forgives
the transgression of the remnant of his inheritance?
You do not stay angry forever but delight to show
mercy. You will again have compassion on us; you
will tread our sins underfoot and hurl all our iniquities
into the depths of the sea. (Micah 7:18–19)

There are many examples of this in the Bible. Before the
apostle Paul came to know the Lord, he did his best to hunt
down believers and destroy the work of Christ. The Bible
tells us that Paul (then called Saul) "breathed out murderous
threats against the Lord's disciples" (Acts 9:1). He even
travelled as far as Damascus to bring the followers of Jesus
to trial in Jerusalem. But on his way to Damascus he met
the Lord Jesus in a magnificent vision. Humanly speaking,
it is hard to understand why God would choose this man to
become one of the greatest missionaries the church has ever
known. Very few mission agencies in our day would risk
accepting such a candidate. Even the church in Jerusalem
found it hard to accept Paul. God, however, saw things
differently. Like Jonah, God offered Paul a second chance.

The apostle Peter understood the forgiveness of God
as well. Too ashamed to admit that he was one of Jesus'
followers, Peter denied that he even knew the Lord just
before he was crucified. A few months later, all the
disciples were gathered together in Jerusalem. The Holy
Spirit fell upon them. On that day, God specifically put
His hand on Peter. He was chosen out of all the disciples
to preach a message that would bring about the conversion
of over three thousand souls. Why did God choose Peter a
second time? He is a God who forgives sin. He is a God of
second chances.

The eighth chapter of John's gospel provides an equally
instructive example of forgiveness. One day, some Pharisees

brought a woman before Jesus, saying she had been found guilty of adultery. Those who brought her to Jesus wanted to know what he thought they should do with her. According to their laws, she deserved to be stoned. Jesus responded to them, "If any one of you is without sin, let him be the first to throw a stone at her" (John 8:7). One by one the men left. While her accusers wanted to kill her, Jesus offered her a second chance.

Each of these people experienced the forgiveness of God in a very real way. Through confession of sin they were each given a second chance. I do not know what you have experienced in life. I do not know what sins you have committed. What I do know, however, is that the Bible teaches that if you confess your sins he will forgive you and offer you a second chance. John makes it perfectly clear in his first epistle: "If we confess our sins, he is faithful and just and will forgive us our sins and purify us from all unrighteousness" (1 John 1:9).

In Christ, you can have a fresh start. By his grace you can wipe the slate clean and start all over again. Jonah was forgiven and given a second chance. Let the Lord do the same for you today.

For Consideration:

- Think about ways in which God has extended his mercy toward you and offered you a second chance. Make a list of some of these second chances.

- Why do you suppose God has given you a second chance?

- What does this teach us about the love of God for us?

- Are there people in your life who you need to forgive and give a second chance? Who are they?

For Prayer:

- Thank God for the many times he did not give up on you but remained faithful despite your rebellion.

- Do you know of someone who is wandering from the Lord today? Ask the Lord to give them a second chance.

- Ask the Lord to reveal to you anyone who you need to forgive and give a second chance.

22
The Repentance of Nineveh

Read Jonah 3:3–4:3

Jonah was given a second chance and this time he obeyed. He had learned his lesson; it was futile to try to resist God.

Once he arrived in Nineveh, Jonah wasted no time announcing that within forty days the city would be destroyed. Jonah never expected the incredible response. Not only did the inhabitants of the city listen to his message, they were convicted of their sins and fell to their knees in repentance.

The Bible tells us that the people of Nineveh believed Jonah and repented of their evil ways. They decreed a general fast in the city, put on mourning clothes, and sat in ashes as signs of humiliation before God. The king himself declared that neither people nor animals should eat or drink. All were commanded to turn from their evil ways and cry out to the God of Jonah for forgiveness. God saw their repentant hearts and as he had done for Jonah, he offered Nineveh a second chance. Through Jonah's ministry, God brought a revival to the Assyrian city of Nineveh.

Have you ever wondered why it was that the Lord so richly blessed the ministry of Jonah? Was it because Jonah had repented of his sin? It doesn't seem likely because Jonah was still far from perfect. Verse 1 of chapter four tells us that when Jonah heard that the Lord was going to forgive Nineveh for her sins, he was not pleased. He wanted the city to be condemned. While he himself had received a second chance, he was unwilling that Nineveh would receive the same opportunity.

Why is it, then, that a single message, preached without compassion, was more fruitful than that which the prophet Jeremiah preached with tears and sorrow for forty years? How many missionaries have worked their whole lives without ever seeing the slightest evidence of fruit? It doesn't seem right that Jonah would see an incredible revival while many greater men saw nothing.

The only answer to this question is found in the sovereign will of God. God does as he pleases with whomever he pleases. When God decided to do a work in the city of Nineveh, he chose to use Jonah in spite of his imperfections. God did not need a sinless prophet to accomplish his purposes. He used Jonah just as he was, imperfect, rebellious, and bitter. He can certainly do the same with us. We must be careful to realize, though, that just because we are being used by God doesn't mean that we are right with God. The story of Jonah is a clear example of this. The secret to success in ministry does not depend on our character, personality, or methods; it depends on God.

It is true that our sin often removes the blessing of God from our lives and ministries. The fact of the matter, however, is that we can be living in a right relationship with God and still, like the prophets of old, see no fruit in our ministry. On the contrary, we cannot say: "I must be living right, look at how God is blessing my ministry." As a sovereign God, he can accomplish his will through a sinner like Jonah or through a great saint like Paul.

Ultimately the advancement of the kingdom of God depends more on God than on man. If God's work depended upon our goodness and spirituality, there would not be much hope for this world. A quick look at the shape of the church in our day ought to prove the validity of this statement. God works despite our imperfections and shortcomings.

For Consideration:

- What comfort do you take from the fact that the work of God goes on despite our shortcomings and failures?

- Does living a good life as a believer necessarily guarantee visible fruit in your life and ministry as a Christian?

- Can we measure how spiritual a person is by how successful their ministry is?

- How does what we learn in this meditation humble us? Upon whom does the success of our ministry depend?

For Prayer:

- Thank the Lord that he can use us in spite of our shortcomings and failures.

- Thank him that he can use you just as you are.

- Ask him to strip you of any pride that leads you to believe that you can achieve what he requires in your own strength.

- Thank him that all your victories have come from him.

23

Jonah's Plant

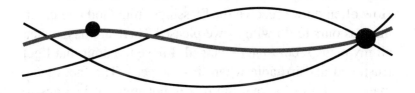

Read Jonah 4:4–11

Jonah could not accept that the Lord had forgiven the people of Nineveh. Finding a place outside the city, he settled down and waited to see what would happen. He was probably still hoping that God would change his mind. As he waited, Jonah made himself a temporary shelter and God graciously caused a plant to grow up around him giving him protection from the scorching sun. Jonah greatly appreciated the shelter of this plant.

While Jonah waited for the judgment of God to fall upon Nineveh, the Lord sent a worm to eat the plant. At the same time, the Lord sent a strong wind and intense heat. Without the shade of the plant, the sun struck Jonah with all its intensity and he weakened under the heat. Jonah cried out to God to take his life because he was angry that the Lord had taken the plant from him.

When asked by God if it was right to be angry about the plant, Jonah responded by telling the Lord that he had every right to be angry, even to the point of death (verse 9). From Jonah's perspective, things couldn't have been any worse. He was in a foreign land. The heat was intolerable. God seemed unjust. As far as Jonah was concerned, the only thing that had gone his way in the last few weeks was to have that plant grow up around him to shelter him from the sun. Now God had even taken that from him.

Notice how Jonah claimed this plant as his own, how he failed to surrender all he had to the Lord. The Lord not only has the right to give, he also has the right to take away. How often do we receive the blessings from God and claim them as ours to do with as we please? There are days when all my plans seem to get changed. I have to admit that I get frustrated and irritable when this happens. The fact of the matter is, however, that the day is not mine. It belongs to the Lord who can choose to do with it as he pleases. Not only must I learn to let God unfold my day as he pleases, I must also learn to let him do whatever he pleases with all the blessings he has given me.

The Lord questions Jonah's concern for the plant. Why had he shown great concern for this plant and no concern whatsoever for the eternal destiny of an entire city? The people had been held in spiritual darkness for so long that they could not distinguish their right from their left. In other words, they did not even know the difference between right and wrong anymore. In reality, the question of God to Jonah was this: "Why are you so concerned about your temporary comforts but completely ignore those who perish all around you?"

The world in which we live resembles the city of Nineveh. It is filled with people who do not know their right from their left. Many people do not know the truth of God. What is our response to this situation? Are we like Jonah, who spent his time wrapped up in his own little world, concerned only about his personal comfort? Why is it that we never have much time for God but plenty of time for our comforts and entertainment? Our possessions are real blessings from God, but they must not take us away from the will of God.

When the children of Israel wandered through the desert, God fed them day after day with manna from heaven. One of the things the Lord told his people was that they were not to take more than they needed for each day. Any manna left over would spoil. In this way they had to rely upon the Lord on a daily basis. God knew human nature was such that it would always be grasping for more. If his people were permitted to accumulate possessions, their lusts would soon get the best of them and nothing else would matter. God himself would soon be cast aside.

The question that each of us must ask ourselves is, "What is our plant?" What is it that consumes our time, energy, and money and takes us away from time in the Word and service for God? Like Jonah's plant, these things will one day be taken from us and we will stand before God to give an account of our lives. How will our priorities measure up to God's expectations? Will they be in tune with the priorities of God?

Jonah's heart was far from God even though God had just used him as an agent of spiritual revival. Even though he was no longer physically running from God, in his heart, he was still running. God had his body and his tongue but he did not have his heart and his will.

Does God have your heart? Does God have your will?

For Consideration:

- Take a moment to think about those things that keep you from the Lord. What is your greatest temptation?

- How much does our society influence us in determining our priorities? Compare the priorities of the Christian with the priorities of the world. What are the differences? What should be the difference?

- What is the difference between God having our body and God having our heart? Does God have your heart?

- What are you willing to sacrifice for the sake of the kingdom of God?

- How do your priorities compare with the priorities of God?

- What do we learn from this passage about God's right over all our possessions?

For Prayer:

- Ask God to help you to have his priorities in life. Surrender your heart to him today.

- Ask God to forgive you for the many times you have put him aside to seek your own will.

- Ask the Lord to open your heart to the needs of others around you. Ask him to lead you in how you are to use your resources for the sake of his kingdom.

Light To My Path
Devotional Commentary Series

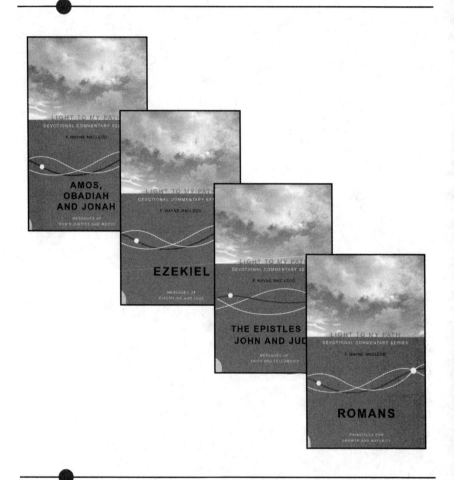

Now Available

Old Testament
- Ezekiel
- Amos, Obadiah, and Jonah

New Testament
- Romans
- The Epistles of John and Jude

A new commentary series for every day devotional use.

- Messages of Discipline and Love

- Messages of God's Justice and Mercy

- Principles for Growth and Maturity

- Messages of Faith and Fellowship

Watch for more in the series
available Fall 2004

Other books available from
Authentic Media . . .

Authentic
MEDIA

PO Box 1047
129 Mobilization Drive
Waynesboro, GA 30830

706-554-1594
1-8MORE-BOOKS
authenticusa@stl.org

An Introduction To The New Testament
Three Volume Collection

D. Edmond Hiebert

Though not a commentary, the Introduction to the New Testament presents each book's message along with a discussion of such questions as authorship, composition, historical circumstances of their writing, issues of criticism and provides helpful, general information on their content and nature. The bibliographies and annotated book list are extremely helpful for pastors, teachers, and laymen as an excellent invitation to further careful exploration.

This book will be prized by all who have a desire to delve deeply into the New Testament writings.

Volume 1: The Gospels And Acts
Volume 2: The Pauline Epistles
Volume 3: The Non-Pauline Epistles and Revelation

1-884543-74-X   976 Pages

Cat and Dog Theology
Rethinking Our Relationship With Our Master

Bob Sjogren & Dr. Gerald Robison

There is a joke about cats and dogs that conveys their differences perfectly.

> A dog says, "You pet me, you feed me, you shelter me, you love me, you must be God."
> A cat says, "You pet me, you feed me, you shelter me, you love me, I must be God."

These God-given traits of cats ("You exist to serve me") and dogs ("I exist to serve you") are often similar to the theological attitudes we have in our view of God and our relationship to Him. Using the differences between cats and dogs in a light-handed manner, the authors compel us to challenge our thinking in deep and profound ways. As you are drawn toward God and the desire to reflect His glory in your life, you will worship, view missions, and pray in a whole new way. This life-changing book will give you a new perspective and vision for God as you delight in the God who delights in you.

1-884543-17-0   206 Pages